Copyright Page

Road to Ramadhaan Preparation Workbook

Copyright © 2024 by [Ri'aayah Institute]

All rights reserved.

No part of this workbook may be reproduced, distributed, or transmitted in any form or by any means, including photocopying, recording, or other electronic or mechanical methods, without the prior written permission of the publisher, except in the case of brief quotations used in a review or other non-commercial uses permitted by copyright law. For permission requests, write to the publisher at the address below:

riaayah.institute@gmail.com

Philadelphia, PA

https://riaayahinstitute.com/

Disclaimer:

This workbook is intended for personal use and spiritual growth. The information provided is based on proofs and evidences from the Qur'aan & Sunnah with the understanding of the Salaf. This book is not a substitute for professional, religious or legal advice. Readers are encouraged to consult with qualified scholars or experts for specific guidance.

Printed in the United States of America

First Edition: 2024

For additional copies or inquiries, contact:

Ri'aayah Institute (riaayah.institute@gmail.com)

May Allaah bless your efforts and grant you success in preparing for Ramadhaan

Aameen.

A Note of Gratitude

In the Name of Allaah, the Most Gracious, the Most Merciful
Alhamdulillaah (All Praise is due to Allaah), and peace blessings be upon our beloved Prophet Muhammad. The completion of this workbook, Road to Ramadhaan Preparation Workbook, would not have been possible without the guidance and blessings of Allaah, the support of dedicated individuals, and the encouragement from the community.

I extend my heartfelt gratitude to everyone who contributed to this project:
To the educators and mentors who provided invaluable insights and ensured the content aligned with Islamic principles.
To the designers, editors, and reviewers who worked diligently to make this workbook engaging and impactful.
To family and friends who offered their unwavering support and encouragement throughout the journey.
And to you, the reader, for embarking on this journey of spiritual growth and preparation for Ramadhaan.
May Allaah Subhanahu wa ta'alaa reward each of you abundantly for your efforts, grant you barakah in your lives, and increase you in goodness, Ameen.

O Allaah, please accept this humble effort as a means to draw closer to You. Let every word, every reflection, and every action inspired by this workbook be a source of guidance, barakah, and forgiveness. Make it a means for those who use it to increase in taqwa (God-consciousness) and strengthen their connection with the Qur'aan and the Sunnah.

O Allaah, grant sincerity in intention and purity in purpose for everyone who contributed to this work. Reward them with the best of this world and the Hereafter, and make this effort a sadaqah jaariyah (continuous charity) that benefits them long after this life.

O Allaah, bless every reader of this workbook. Open their hearts to Your guidance, ease their journey through Ramadhaan, and accept their fasting, prayers, and good deeds. Let this workbook serve as a means to transform hearts and lives.

May peace and blessing be upon our beloved Prophet Muhammad, his family and those that follow him Aameen!

Table of Contents

How to Use This Workbook 5

Introduction 8

The Virtues of Supplication 13

Etiquette's of Supplicating That Lead to Dua Being Answered 14

Times, Circumstances and Places Supplications are Answered 33

Week 1 40

Reflections 69

Week 2 93

Intentions & Goal Setting 124

Table of Contents

Week 3 135

Practical Tips for Fasting Preparation 165

Week 4 184

Health & Wellness Tips 204

Week 5 254

Weekly Meal Planners 275

Week 6 282

Trackers 301

How to Use This Workbook

Welcome to Your Road to Ramadhaan Preparation Workbook! This workbook is designed to guide you step-by-step in preparing spiritually, mentally, and physically for the blessed month of Ramadhaan. It provides tools, reflections, and trackers to help you make the most of this transformative time.
Here's how to use each section of the workbook:

Reflection Prompts:
- Start your journey by reflecting on your spiritual and personal goals. Use the provided prompts to uncover areas of improvement and align your actions with your intentions.
- Set aside time weekly to review your answers and adjust your focus as needed.

Goals and Intention Setting:
- Use the SMART goals framework to set clear, actionable objectives for Ramadhaan.
- Divide your goals into spiritual, personal, and community categories, and track them using the progress tracker.

Practical Tips for Fasting Preparation:
- Follow the tips to adjust your sleep routine, plan balanced meals, and gradually ease into fasting. These practical steps will make your transition into Ramadhaan smoother and more effective.

How to Use This Workbook

Names of Allaah Memorization:
- Dedicate time to learning the beautiful names of Allaah (Asma'ul Husna). {Recommended read: Shaykh 'Abdur Razzaaq 'Abdul Muhsin al Badr حفظه الله}
- Memorize one to three names a day (based on the weekly plan), reflecting on their meanings and how they apply to your life.
- Use the provided pages to write where you can find that name in the Qur'aan or Sunnah.
- Use the provided notes pages to write important notes or to duplicate the Names of Allaah to help with memorization.
- Use the provided tracker to monitor your progress.

Sustainable Habits Tracker:
- Develop and track habits such as daily Qur'aan reading, Sunnah prayers, dhikr, and acts of kindness.
- Use the habit tracker to ensure consistency and reflect on what works best for you.

Qur'aan Reading Tracker:
- Complete the Qur'aan during Ramadhaan by following the structured plan of reading five pages after each prayer.
- Track your progress daily and reflect on the insights you gain from the Qur'aan.

Health, Wellness, and Habit-Building Tips:
- Incorporate physical, mental, and spiritual practices to maintain your energy and focus throughout Ramadhaan.
- Use the health tips to plan balanced meals, stay hydrated, and optimize your sleep schedule.

How to Use This Workbook

Dua Memorization Tracker:
- Track your progress in memorizing key supplications for Ramadhaan, including those for Suhoor, Iftar, and Laylatul Qadr.
- Reflect on how these supplications enhance your connection with Allaah.
- Use the provided notes pages to write important notes or to duplicate the supplication to help with memorization.
- Use the provided tracker to monitor your progress.

Weekly Reflection Pages:
- At the end of each week, use the reflection prompts to evaluate your progress, identify areas of growth, and plan for the next week.
- Write down your insights and use them to adjust your goals and intentions.

Tips for Success:
- Set aside a dedicated time each day to work on your workbook.
- Be honest with yourself during reflections and goal-setting.
- Use the trackers and tables to monitor your progress and celebrate your achievements.
- Remember that consistency is more important than perfection. Small, steady steps will lead to meaningful growth.

This workbook is your companion on the journey to a spiritually fulfilling and transformative Ramadhaan. May Allaah grant you barakah in your efforts and accept all your deeds. Aameen.

Introduction

In the Name of Allaah, The Most Merciful, The Most Beneficent
Indeed, all praise is due to Allaah. We praise Him, seek His aid, ask for His forgiveness and repent to Him. We seek refuge with Allaah from the evil of our own souls and the evil of our wicked actions. Whomsoever Allaah guides, then none can guide; and whomsoever Allaah misguides, then none can guide.

I testify that none has the right to be worshiped except Allaah alone without any partner, and I testify that Muhammad is His Slave and Messenger, may an abundant of peace and blessings be upon him, his family, and all of his companions.

To Proceed:
Our pious predecessors (Salafunaa As Saalih) would begin their preparation months in advance, to reap the maximum benefit from Ramadhaan. Rather, they realized that, beginning with Rajab, they had seven months of blessing in front of them to strengthen their closeness and connection with Allaah.

He, the Sublime and Exalted states:

إِنَّ عِدَّةَ الشُّهُورِ عِنْدَ اللَّهِ اثْنَا عَشَرَ شَهْراً فِي كِتَابِ اللَّهِ يَوْمَ خَلَقَ السَّمَاوَاتِ وَالْأَرْضَ مِنْهَا أَرْبَعَةٌ حُرُمٌ ذَلِكَ الدِّينُ الْقَيِّمُ} [التوبة: ٣٦] {فَلَا تَظْلِمُوا فِيهِنَّ أَنْفُسَكُمْ

{Verily, the number of months with Allaah is twelve months (in a year), so was it ordained by Allaah on the Day when He created the heavens and the earth; of them four are Sacred (i.e. the 1st, the 7th, the 11th and the 12th months of the Islâmic calendar). That is the right religion, so wrong not yourselves therein...} At-Tawbah:36

Explaining this ayah, Allaah's Messenger (ﷺ) said in his famous farewell speech:

"إن الزمان قد استدار كهيئته يوم خلق الله السماوات والأرض السنة اثنا عشر شهرا منها أربعة حرم ثلاثة متواليات: ذو القعدة وذو الحجة والمحرم ورجب مضر الذي بين جمادى وشعبان"

The year consists of twelve months, of which four are sacred; three of them are consecutive: Dhu al-Qi'dah, Dhu al-Hijjah, Muharram, and Rajab of Mudar which comes between the months of Jumāda and Sha'bān.

Consequently, starting from the 7th month of the lunar Hijri calendar, we have:
7- Rajab (Sacred)
8- Sha'baan
9- Ramadhan
10- Shawwaal
11- Dthul Qi'dah (Sacred)
12- Dthul Hijjah (Sacred)
1- Muharram (Sacred)

These seven consecutive months were referred to by our Salaf as the Seasons of Good (Mawaasim Al Khayr)

The illustrious scholar Ibn Rajab Al Hanbali (Allaah's Mercy be upon him) authored an entire treatise on this very topic, entitled:

'Subtle Points of Knowledge Regarding the Blessed Opportunities Hidden in each Season of the Year (Lataaif Al- Ma'arifah fee Maa li Mawasim Al 'Aam minal wadthaaif).

In this book, he details the blessed opportunities for righteous increase in each of these months, or seasons within the Hijri year.

Rajab and Sha'baan are two blessed months used by the righteous, both past and present, to focus on purification and self-correction, to reap maximum benefit from the blessed month of Ramadhan.

In this regard, Ibn Rajab stated:
The month of Rajab is the door opener to (seven) months of goodness and blessing.

As Abu Bakr Al Warraaq Al Balkhee said,
"Rajab is the month to sow seeds, Sha'baan is to irrigate them, and Ramadhan is to reap the growth.

قال أبو بكر الوراق البلخي: شهر رجب شهر للزرع ، وشعبان شهر السقي للزرع ، ورمضان شهر حصاد الزرع

He also said, "Rajab is the blessed winds, Sha'baan is the heavy cloud formulation, and Ramadhaan is the blessed rain pour".

وعنه قال: مثل شهر رجب مثل الريح ، ومثل شعبان مثل الغيم ، ومثل رمضان مثل القطر

Another Salaf said, "The year is like a tree if cared for properly. In Rajab, it's leaves sprout forth... in Sha'baan, its fruits grow... and in Ramadhan, the believers partake from its fruit."

In Rajab, each of us should take full opportunity to self-correct by:

- Leaving off any bad habits acquired during the preceding months

- Seeking sincere forgiveness

- Replacing unsavory habits with righteous ones...

Then, in Sha'baan, pay extra attention to consistency and perfection of your righteous deeds so that in Ramadhaan, we can continue upon our corrected ways and reap an exponential reward and an increase of Allaah's Mercy, Guidance, and Blessing in the year to come.

The scholars unanimously agree that there are no deeds specifically legislated to perform during the month of Rajab. That being clarified, there is a plethora of righteous habits they recommend to begin to perfect during both Rajab and Sha'baan. Of them:

1- Guarding the 5 obligatory prayers, each at its beginning time

Abdullah asked the Prophet Muhammad (ﷺ), "Which deed is the dearest to Allaah?" He replied, "To offer the prayers at their early stated fixed times." (Sahih al-Bukhari 527).

2- Guarding the 12 sunnah raka'at connected to the obligatory prayers:

Allaah will build a house in Paradise for whoever is diligent in observing 12 Sunnah Raka'at (as follows): 4 Rak'at before and 2 after the Dhuhr (Midday) Prayer, 2 after the Maghrib (Sunset Prayer), 2 after the 'Isha (Evening) Prayer and 2 before the Fajr (Dawn) Prayer." (Sunan Ibn Majah 1140)

3- Guarding the Duha Prayer

The Messenger of Allaah (ﷺ) said: "No one persists in offering Duha prayer except an Awwaab (one who often turns to Allaah), for it is the prayer of those who often turn to Allaah (salat al-awwabin)."

4- Guard the late night prayer (Qiyam Al- Layl)

And he said: "You should pray qiyam al-layl, for it is the custom of the righteous who came before you, and it brings you closer to your Lord, and expiates sins and prevents misdeeds." Narrated by al-Tirmidhi, 3549; classed as Hasan by al-Albaani in Irwa' al-Ghaleel, 452.

5- Salatul Witr

Allaah's Messenger (ﷺ) said, "The night prayer is offered as two raka'at followed by two raka'at and so on and if anyone is afraid of the approaching dawn (Fajr prayer) he should pray one raka'ah, and this will be a Witr for all the raka'ah which he has prayed before."

6- Constant Dhikr (Remembrance) of Allaah

Abdullah ibn Busr reported: A man said, "O Messenger of Allaah, the laws of Islam are too many for me, so tell me something I can hold onto." The Messenger of Allaah (ﷺ), said, "Keep your tongue moist with the remembrance of Allaah."
(Sunan al-Tirmidhī 3375)
Grade: Sahih (authentic) according to Al-Albani

7- Reading/reciting the Qur'aan with deep contemplation

Allaah, the Exalted, said:

{ أفلا يتدبرون القرآن أم على قلوب أقفالها }

{Will they not then reflect upon the Qur'an, or are there locks upon their hearts}
Surah Muhammad: 24

8- Ad Du'aa (Supplicating to Allaah)

Allaah said,

﴿وَقَالَ رَبُّكُمُ ادْعُونِي أَسْتَجِبْ لَكُمْ إِنَّ الَّذِينَ يَسْتَكْبِرُونَ عَنْ عِبَادَتِي سَيَدْخُلُونَ جَهَنَّمَ دَاخِرِينَ﴾

Your Lord has said: 'Call on Me and I will answer you. Those who are too proud to worship Me shall enter Hellfire in humiliation!' (Ghafir: 60)

9- Giving charity

The Messenger of Allaah (ﷺ) said: "Allaah said: 'Spend, O son of Adam, and I shall spend on you.'"
Narrated by al-Bukhari, 5073; Muslim, 993.
The Prophet (ﷺ) said "Sadaqah extinguishes sin as water extinguishes fire". (At-Tirmidhi 614)

10- Seeking Allaah's forgiveness, constantly

Allaah, the Exalted, says:
"So know (O Muhammad – ﷺ) that La ilaha ill-Allah (none has the right to be worshipped but Allaah), and ask forgiveness for your sin, and also for (the sin of) believing men and believing women."
[Muhammad 47: 19].

The goal is to replace previous time wasting habits with righteous deeds and increase in Allaah's Pleasure until we meet Him, pleased with us, and us with Him.

May Allaah bless us with introspection and self correction in Rajab and Sha'baan, and have us achieve the most success in Ramadhan.

فضيلة الدعاء
The Virtue of Supplication

Supplicating to our Lord سبحانه وتعالى has many virtues. Allaah عز وجل states:

﴿ وَقَالَ رَبُّكُمُ ادْعُونِي أَسْتَجِبْ لَكُمْ ﴾ غافر ٦٠

"And your Lord says, "Call upon Me; I will respond to you." Ghaafir: 60

﴿وَإِذَا سَأَلَكَ عِبَادِي عَنِّي فَإِنِّي قَرِيبٌ ۖ أُجِيبُ دَعْوَةَ الدَّاعِ إِذَا دَعَانِ ۖ فَلْيَسْتَجِيبُوا لِي وَلْيُؤْمِنُوا بِي لَعَلَّهُمْ يَرْشُدُونَ﴾ البقرة ١٨٦

"And when My servants ask you, [O Muhammad], concerning Me - indeed I am near. I respond to the invocation of the supplicant when he calls upon Me. So let them respond to Me [by obedience] and believe in Me that they may be [rightly] guided." Baqarah: 186

Allaah tells us that he is near and to call upon Him, and he will answer us! Supplicating is an act of worship that we shouldn't take lightly.

حَدَّثَنَا حَفْصُ بْنُ عُمَرَ، حَدَّثَنَا شُعْبَةُ، عَنْ مَنْصُورٍ، عَنْ ذَرٍّ، عَنْ يُسَيْعٍ الْحَضْرَمِيِّ، عَنِ النُّعْمَانِ بْنِ بَشِيرٍ، عَنِ النَّبِيِّ صلى الله عليه وسلم قَالَ " الدُّعَاءُ هُوَ الْعِبَادَةُ

{ قَالَ رَبُّكُمُ ادْعُونِي أَسْتَجِبْ لَكُمْ }

حكم: صحيح (الألباني)

سنن أبي داود ١٤٧٩

Narrated An-Nu'man ibn Bashir: The Prophet ﷺ said: Supplication (du'a') is worship. (He then recited: "And your Lord said: Call on Me, I will answer you" Sunan Abi Dawud 1479

Etiquette's of Supplicating That Lead to Dua Being Answered

آداب الدعاء التي تؤدي إلى إجابة الدعاء

١- الإخلاص:

Sincerity to Allaah by calling upon Him alone.

﴿فَادْعُوا اللَّهَ مُخْلِصِينَ لَهُ الدِّينَ وَلَوْ كَرِهَ الْكَافِرُونَ﴾ غافر ١٤

Allah (ﷻ) said: "So invoke Allaah, [being] sincere to Him in religion, although the disbelievers dislike it."

٢- ابد الدعاء بحمد الله والشكر له ثم صلّ على النبي ﷺ

Begin the supplication with praising Allaah and expressing gratitude toward him, then sending salutations upon the Prophet ﷺ.

عَنْ فَضَالَةَ بْنِ عُبَيْدٍ، قَالَ بَيْنَا رَسُولُ اللَّهِ صلى الله عليه وسلم قَاعِدًا إِذْ دَخَلَ رَجُلٌ فَصَلَّى فَقَالَ اللَّهُمَّ اغْفِرْ لِي وَارْحَمْنِي . فَقَالَ رَسُولُ اللَّهِ صلى الله عليه وسلم " عَجِلْتَ أَيُّهَا الْمُصَلِّي إِذَا صَلَّيْتَ فَقَعَدْتَ فَاحْمَدِ اللَّهَ بِمَا هُوَ أَهْلُهُ وَصَلِّ عَلَىَّ ثُمَّ ادْعُهُ " . قَالَ ثُمَّ صَلَّى رَجُلٌ آخَرُ بَعْدَ ذَلِكَ فَحَمِدَ اللَّهَ وَصَلَّى عَلَى النَّبِيِّ صلى الله عليه وسلم فَقَالَ لَهُ النَّبِيُّ صلى الله عليه وسلم " أَيُّهَا الْمُصَلِّي ادْعُ تُجَبْ " . الترمذي ٣٤٧٦ حكم: حسن

Fadalah bin `Ubaid narrated:

"While the Messenger of Allaah ﷺ was seated, a man entered and performed Salat, and he said: 'O Allaah, forgive me, and have mercy upon me.' The Messenger of Allaah ﷺ said: 'You have rushed, O praying person. When you perform Salat and then sit, then praise Allaah with what He is deserving of, and send Salat upon me, then call upon Him.'" He said: "Then another man performed Salat after that, so he praised Allaah and sent Salat upon the Prophet ﷺ. The Prophet ﷺ said to him: 'O praying person! Supplicate, and you shall be answered.'" (At-Tirmidhi 3476)

٣- كن حازمًا في الدعاء بلا تردد وتأكد من أنك ستتلقى ردًا بطريقة أو بأخرى
Be assertive/determined in supplicating, without hesitation and be certain that you'll receive a response in one way or another.

عَنْ أَبِي هُرَيْرَةَ، أَنَّ رَسُولَ اللَّهِ صلى الله عليه وسلم قَالَ "لاَ يَقُولَنَّ أَحَدُكُمُ اللَّهُمَّ اغْفِرْ لِي إِنْ شِئْتَ اللَّهُمَّ ارْحَمْنِي إِنْ شِئْتَ لِيَعْزِمِ الْمَسْأَلَةَ فَإِنَّهُ لاَ مُكْرِهَ لَهُ " الترمذي ٣٤٩٧

حكم: صحيح

Abu Hurairah narrated that the Messenger of Allaah ﷺ said: "None of you should say: 'O Allah forgive me if You wish. O Allaah have mercy on me if You wish.' Let him be firm in asking, for there is none that can compel Him to do things." At-Tirmidhi 3497

٤- ثابر على دعاء الله بالدعاء ولا تكن متسرعا أو جزعا
Be persistent in calling upon Allaah with dua and do not be hasty or impatient.

عَنْ أَبِي هُرَيْرَةَ، عَنِ النَّبِيِّ صلى الله عليه وسلم قَالَ " يُسْتَجَابُ لأَحَدِكُمْ مَا لَمْ يَعْجَلْ يَقُولُ دَعَوْتُ فَلَمْ يُسْتَجَبْ لِي " الترمذي ٣٣٨٧

حكم: صحيح

Abu Hurairah narrated that the Prophet ﷺ said: "One of you will be responded to, so long as he is not hasty, saying: 'I supplicated, and I was not responded to.'" At-Tirmidhi 3387

٥- أن يكون له عقل ومنتبه القلب أثناء الدعاء
Have presence/consciousness and alertness of the heart during supplicating.

عَنْ أَبِي هُرَيْرَةَ، قَالَ قَالَ رَسُولُ اللَّهِ صلى الله عليه وسلم " ادْعُوا اللَّهَ وَأَنْتُمْ مُوقِنُونَ بِالإِجَابَةِ وَاعْلَمُوا أَنَّ اللَّهَ لاَ يَسْتَجِيبُ دُعَاءً مِنْ قَلْبٍ غَافِلٍ لاَهٍ. الترمذي ٣٤٧٩

حكم: صحيح الألباني

Abu Hurairah narrated that the Messenger of Allaah ﷺ said: "Call upon Allaah while being certain of being answered, and know that Allaah does not respond to a supplication from the heart of one heedless and occupied by play." At-Tirmidhi 3479

٦- ادع إلى الله في أوقات السهولة فيجيب في أوقات الشدائد

Supplicate to Allaah in times of ease, and He will answer during times of hardship. Do not only call on Allaah during times of hardship.

عَنْ أَبِي هُرَيْرَةَ، رضي الله عنه قَالَ: قَالَ رَسُولُ اللَّهِ ﷺ " مَنْ سَرَّهُ أَنْ يَسْتَجِيبَ اللَّهُ لَهُ عِنْدَ الشَّدَائِدِ وَالْكُرَبِ فَلْيُكْثِرِ الدُّعَاءَ فِي الرَّخَاءِ " الترمذي ٣٣٨٢

Abu Huraira reported: The Messenger of Allaah (ﷺ) said, "Whoever would be pleased for Allaah to answer him during times of hardship and difficulty, let him supplicate often during times of ease." At-Tirmidhi 3382

٧- لا تسأل من غير الله وتتوكل عليه تماما

Do not ask from anyone other than Allaah, and rely on Him totally.

عَنِ ابْنِ عَبَّاسٍ، قَالَ كُنْتُ خَلْفَ رَسُولِ اللَّهِ صلى الله عليه وسلم يَوْمًا فَقَالَ " يَا غُلاَمُ إِنِّي أُعَلِّمُكَ كَلِمَاتٍ احْفَظِ اللَّهَ يَحْفَظْكَ احْفَظِ اللَّهَ تَجِدْهُ تُجَاهَكَ إِذَا سَأَلْتَ فَاسْأَلِ اللَّهَ وَإِذَا اسْتَعَنْتَ فَاسْتَعِنْ بِاللَّهِ وَاعْلَمْ أَنَّ الأُمَّةَ لَوِ اجْتَمَعَتْ عَلَى أَنْ يَنْفَعُوكَ بِشَيْءٍ لَمْ يَنْفَعُوكَ إِلاَّ بِشَيْءٍ قَدْ كَتَبَهُ اللَّهُ لَكَ وَلَوِ اجْتَمَعُوا عَلَى أَنْ يَضُرُّوكَ بِشَيْءٍ لَمْ يَضُرُّوكَ إِلاَّ بِشَيْءٍ قَدْ كَتَبَهُ اللَّهُ عَلَيْكَ رُفِعَتِ الأَقْلاَمُ وَجَفَّتِ الصُّحُفُ " الترمذي ٢٥١٦ حكم: حسن

Ibn 'Abbas narrated: "I was behind the Prophet ﷺ one day when he said: 'O boy! I will teach you a statement: Be mindful of Allaah and He will protect you. Be mindful of Allaah and you will find Him before you. When you ask, ask Allaah, and when you seek aid, seek Allaah's aid. Know that if the entire creation were to gather together to do something to benefit you- you would never get any benefit except that Allaah had written for you. And if they were to gather to do something to harm you- you would never be harmed except that Allah had written for you. The pens are lifted, and the pages are dried.'" At-Tirmidhi 2516

٨- لا تدعوا تجاه أهلكم ومالكم
Do not supplicate against your family or your wealth.

عَنْ جَابِرِ بْنِ عَبْدِ اللَّهِ، قَالَ قَالَ رَسُولُ اللَّهِ صلى الله عليه وسلم " لاَ تَدْعُوا عَلَى أَنْفُسِكُمْ وَلاَ تَدْعُوا عَلَى أَوْلاَدِكُمْ وَلاَ تَدْعُوا عَلَى خَدَمِكُمْ وَلاَ تَدْعُوا عَلَى أَمْوَالِكُمْ لاَ تُوَافِقُوا مِنَ اللَّهِ تَبَارَكَ وَتَعَالَى سَاعَةَ نَيْلٍ فِيهَا عَطَاءٌ فَيَسْتَجِيبَ لَكُمْ " سنن أبي داود ١٥٣٢ حكم: صحيح الألباني

Jabir b. 'Abd Allah reported the Messenger of Allaah ﷺ as saying:
"Do not invoke curse on yourselves, and do not invoke curse on your children, and do not invoke curse on your servants, and do not invoke curse on your property, lest you happen to do it at a time when Allaah is asked for something and grants your request." Sunan Abi Dawud 1532

٩- تدعوا في نبرة معتدلة
Supplicate in a moderate tone (somewhere between quiet and audible)

﴿ ادْعُوا رَبَّكُمْ تَضَرُّعًا وَخُفْيَةً ۚ إِنَّهُ لَا يُحِبُّ الْمُعْتَدِينَ ﴾ الأعراف ٥٥

Allaah ﷻ says "Call upon your Lord in humility and privately; indeed, He does not like transgressors/aggressors." Al-A'raaf: 55

عَنْ أَبِي مُوسَى، قَالَ كُنَّا مَعَ النَّبِيِّ صلى الله عليه وسلم فِي سَفَرٍ فَجَعَلَ النَّاسُ يَجْهَرُونَ بِالتَّكْبِيرِ فَقَالَ النَّبِيُّ صلى الله عليه وسلم " أَيُّهَا النَّاسُ ارْبَعُوا عَلَى أَنْفُسِكُمْ إِنَّكُمْ لَيْسَ تَدْعُونَ أَصَمَّ وَلاَ غَائِبًا إِنَّكُمْ تَدْعُونَ سَمِيعًا قَرِيبًا وَهُوَ مَعَكُمْ " . قَالَ وَأَنَا خَلْفَهُ وَأَنَا أَقُولُ لاَ حَوْلَ وَلاَ قُوَّةَ إِلاَّ بِاللَّهِ فَقَالَ " يَا عَبْدَ اللَّهِ بْنَ قَيْسٍ أَلاَ أَدُلُّكَ عَلَى كَنْزٍ مِنْ كُنُوزِ الْجَنَّةِ " . فَقُلْتُ بَلَى يَا رَسُولَ اللَّهِ . قَالَ " قُلْ لاَ حَوْلَ وَلاَ قُوَّةَ إِلاَّ بِاللَّهِ " مسلم ٢٧٠٤

Abu Musa reported: We were along with Allaah's Apostle ﷺ on a journey when the people began to pronounce "Allaahu Akbar" in a loud voice. Thereupon Allaah's Messenger ﷺ said: O people, show mercy to yourselves, for you are not calling One who is deaf or absent. Verily, you are calling One who is All-Hearing (and) Near to you and is with you. Abu Musa said that he had been behind him (the Prophet) and recited: "There is neither might nor power but that of Allaah." He (the Prophet), while addressing 'Abdullah b. Qais, said: Should I not direct you to a treasure from amongst the treasures of Paradise? I ('Abdullah b. Qais) said: Allaah's Messenger, do it, of course. Thereupon he (the Prophet) said: Then recite: "There is no might and no power but that of Allaah." Muslim 2704

١٠- ادعوا الله بأسمائه الحسنى الصفات السامية
Supplicate to Allaah by His beautiful names and lofty attributes

﴿وَلِلَّهِ الْأَسْمَاءُ الْحُسْنَىٰ فَادْعُوهُ بِهَا ۖ وَذَرُوا الَّذِينَ يُلْحِدُونَ فِي أَسْمَائِهِ ۚ سَيُجْزَوْنَ مَا كَانُوا يَعْمَلُونَ﴾ الأعراف ١٨٠

Allaah says, "And to Allah belong the best names, so invoke Him by them. And leave [the company of] those who practice deviation concerning His names. They will be recompensed for what they have been doing." Al-A'raaf: 180

١١- قبول ذنوبك والثبات في فضل الله تعالى
Accepting your sins and affirming Allaah's bounty

شَدَّادُ بْنُ أَوْسٍ ـ رضى الله عنه ـ عَنِ النَّبِيِّ صلى الله عليه وسلم " سَيِّدُ الاِسْتِغْفَارِ أَنْ تَقُولَ اللَّهُمَّ أَنْتَ رَبِّي، لاَ إِلَهَ إِلاَّ أَنْتَ، خَلَقْتَنِي وَأَنَا عَبْدُكَ، وَأَنَا عَلَى عَهْدِكَ وَوَعْدِكَ مَا اسْتَطَعْتُ، أَعُوذُ بِكَ مِنْ شَرِّ مَا صَنَعْتُ، أَبُوءُ لَكَ بِنِعْمَتِكَ عَلَىَّ وَأَبُوءُ لَكَ بِذَنْبِي، فَاغْفِرْ لِي، فَإِنَّهُ لاَ يَغْفِرُ الذُّنُوبَ إِلاَّ أَنْتَ ". قَالَ " وَمَنْ قَالَهَا مِنَ النَّهَارِ مُوقِنًا بِهَا، فَمَاتَ مِنْ يَوْمِهِ قَبْلَ أَنْ يُمْسِيَ، فَهُوَ مِنْ أَهْلِ الْجَنَّةِ، وَمَنْ قَالَهَا مِنَ اللَّيْلِ وَهُوَ مُوقِنٌ بِهَا، فَمَاتَ قَبْلَ أَنْ يُصْبِحَ، فَهُوَ مِنْ أَهْلِ الْجَنَّةِ ".

البخاري ٦٣٠٦

Narrated Shaddad bin Aus: The Prophet ﷺ said "The most superior way of asking for forgiveness from Allaah is: 'Allaahumma anta Rabbi la ilaha illa anta, Khalaqtani wa ana `Abduka, wa ana `ala `ahdika wa wa`dika mastata`tu, A`udhu bika min Sharri ma sana`tu, abu'u Laka bini`matika `alaiya, wa abu'u laka bidhanbi faghfir lee fa innahu la yaghfiru adhdhunuba illa anta." The Prophet ﷺ added. "If somebody recites it during the day with firm faith in it, and dies on the same day before the evening, he will be from the people of Paradise; and if somebody recites it at night with firm faith in it, and dies before the morning, he will be from the people of Paradise." Al-Bukhari 6306

١٢- الامتناع عن استعمال القوافي عند الدعاء
Refraining from rhyming when making supplication

عَنْ عِكْرِمَةَ، عَنِ ابْنِ عَبَّاسٍ، قَالَ حَدِّثِ النَّاسَ، كُلَّ جُمُعَةٍ مَرَّةً، فَإِنْ أَبَيْتَ فَمَرَّتَيْنِ، فَإِنْ أَكْثَرْتَ فَثَلاَثَ مِرَارٍ وَلاَ تُمِلَّ النَّاسَ هَذَا الْقُرْآنَ، وَلاَ أُلْفِيَنَّكَ تَأْتِي الْقَوْمَ وَهُمْ فِي حَدِيثٍ مِنْ حَدِيثِهِمْ فَتَقُصُّ عَلَيْهِمْ، فَتَقْطَعَ عَلَيْهِمْ حَدِيثَهُمْ فَتُمِلَّهُمْ، وَلَكِنْ أَنْصِتْ، فَإِذَا أَمَرُوكَ فَحَدِّثْهُمْ وَهُمْ يَشْتَهُونَهُ، فَانْظُرِ السَّجْعَ مِنَ الدُّعَاءِ فَاجْتَنِبْهُ، فَإِنِّي عَهِدْتُ رَسُولَ اللَّهِ صلى الله عليه وسلم وَأَصْحَابَهُ لاَ يَفْعَلُونَ إِلاَّ ذَلِكَ. يَعْنِي لاَ يَفْعَلُونَ إِلاَّ ذَلِكَ الاِجْتِنَابَ. البخاري ٦٣٣٧

Narrated `Ikrima: Ibn `Abbas said, "Preach to the people once a week, and if you won't, then preach them twice, but if you want to preach more, then let it be three times (a week only), and do not make the people fed-up with this Qur'aan. If you come to some people who are engaged in a talk, don't start interrupting their talk by preaching, lest you should cause them to be bored. You should rather keep quiet, and if they ask you, then preach to them at the time when they are eager to hear what you say. And avoid the use of rhymed prose in invocation for I noticed that Allaah's Messenger ﷺ and his companions always avoided it."

NOTES:

NOTES:

NOTES:

١٣- ادعوا إلى الله بالتواضع والمطيع والرغبة والخوف
Supplicate to Allaah with humility, submissiveness, desire and fear

﴿وَاذْكُر رَّبَّكَ فِي نَفْسِكَ تَضَرُّعًا وَخِيفَةً وَدُونَ الْجَهْرِ مِنَ الْقَوْلِ بِالْغُدُوِّ وَالْآصَالِ وَلَا تَكُن مِّنَ الْغَافِلِينَ﴾ الأعراف ٢٠٥

And remember your Lord within yourself, humbly and fearfully, and quietly, in the morning and the evening, and do not be of the neglectful. Al-A'raaf 205

﴿فَاسْتَجَبْنَا لَهُ وَوَهَبْنَا لَهُ يَحْيَىٰ وَأَصْلَحْنَا لَهُ زَوْجَهُ ۚ إِنَّهُمْ كَانُوا يُسَارِعُونَ فِي الْخَيْرَاتِ وَيَدْعُونَنَا رَغَبًا وَرَهَبًا ۖ وَكَانُوا لَنَا خَاشِعِينَ﴾ الأنبياء ٩٠

So, We answered his call, and We bestowed upon him Yahya (John), and cured his wife (so then she could bear a child) for him. Verily, they used to hasten on to do good deeds, and they used to call on Us with hope and fear and used to humble themselves before Us. Al-Anbiya: 90

١٤- ادعوا إلى الله بالعمل الصالح
Supplicate to Allaah through righteous deeds

عَنِ ابْنِ عُمَرَ ـ رضى الله عنهما ـ عَنِ النَّبِيِّ صلى الله عليه وسلم قَالَ " خَرَجَ ثَلاَثَةٌ يَمْشُونَ فَأَصَابَهُمُ الْمَطَرُ، فَدَخَلُوا فِي غَارٍ فِي جَبَلٍ، فَانْحَطَّتْ عَلَيْهِمْ صَخْرَةٌ. قَالَ فَقَالَ بَعْضُهُمْ لِبَعْضٍ ادْعُوا اللَّهَ بِأَفْضَلِ عَمَلٍ عَمِلْتُمُوهُ. فَقَالَ أَحَدُهُمُ اللَّهُمَّ، إِنِّي كَانَ لِي أَبَوَانِ شَيْخَانِ كَبِيرَانِ، فَكُنْتُ أَخْرُجُ فَأَرْعَى، ثُمَّ أَجِيءُ فَأَحْلُبُ، فَأَجِيءُ بِالْحِلاَبِ فَآتِي بِهِ أَبَوَىَّ فَيَشْرَبَانِ، ثُمَّ أَسْقِي الصِّبْيَةَ وَأَهْلِي وَامْرَأَتِي، فَاحْتَبَسْتُ لَيْلَةً. فَجِئْتُ فَإِذَا هُمَا نَائِمَانِ ـ قَالَ ـ فَكَرِهْتُ أَنْ أُوقِظَهُمَا، وَالصِّبْيَةُ يَتَضَاغَوْنَ عِنْدَ رِجْلَىَّ، فَلَمْ يَزَلْ ذَلِكَ دَأْبِي وَدَأْبُهُمَا، حَتَّى طَلَعَ الْفَجْرُ اللَّهُمَّ إِنْ كُنْتَ تَعْلَمُ أَنِّي فَعَلْتُ ذَلِكَ ابْتِغَاءَ وَجْهِكَ فَافْرُجْ عَنَّا فُرْجَةً نَرَى مِنْهَا السَّمَاءَ. قَالَ فَفُرِجَ عَنْهُمْ. وَقَالَ الآخَرُ اللَّهُمَّ إِنْ كُنْتَ تَعْلَمُ أَنِّي كُنْتُ أُحِبُّ امْرَأَةً مِنْ بَنَاتِ عَمِّي كَأَشَدِّ مَا يُحِبُّ الرَّجُلُ النِّسَاءَ، فَقَالَتْ لاَ تَنَالُ ذَلِكَ مِنْهَا حَتَّى تُعْطِيَهَا مِائَةَ دِينَارٍ. فَسَعَيْتُ فِيهَا حَتَّى جَمَعْتُهَا، فَلَمَّا قَعَدْتُ بَيْنَ رِجْلَيْهَا قَالَتِ اتَّقِ اللَّهَ، وَلاَ تَفُضَّ الْخَاتَمَ إِلاَّ بِحَقِّهِ. فَقُمْتُ وَتَرَكْتُهَا، فَإِنْ كُنْتَ تَعْلَمُ أَنِّي فَعَلْتُ ذَلِكَ ابْتِغَاءَ وَجْهِكَ فَافْرُجْ عَنَّا فُرْجَةً. قَالَ فَفَرَجَ عَنْهُمُ الثُّلُثَيْنِ. وَقَالَ الآخَرُ اللَّهُمَّ إِنْ كُنْتَ تَعْلَمُ أَنِّي اسْتَأْجَرْتُ أَجِيرًا بِفَرَقٍ مِنْ ذُرَةٍ فَأَعْطَيْتُهُ، وَأَبَى ذَاكَ أَنْ يَأْخُذَ، فَعَمَدْتُ إِلَى ذَلِكَ الْفَرَقِ، فَزَرَعْتُهُ حَتَّى اشْتَرَيْتُ مِنْهُ بَقَرًا وَرَاعِيَهَا، ثُمَّ جَاءَ فَقَالَ يَا عَبْدَ اللَّهِ أَعْطِنِي حَقِّي. فَقُلْتُ انْطَلِقْ إِلَى تِلْكَ الْبَقَرِ وَرَاعِيهَا، فَإِنَّهَا لَكَ. فَقَالَ أَتَسْتَهْزِئُ بِي. فَقَالَ فَقُلْتُ مَا أَسْتَهْزِئُ بِكَ وَلَكِنَّهَا لَكَ. اللَّهُمَّ إِنْ كُنْتَ تَعْلَمُ أَنِّي فَعَلْتُ ذَلِكَ ابْتِغَاءَ وَجْهِكَ فَافْرُجْ عَنَّا. فَكُشِفَ عَنْهُمْ " البخاري ٢٢١٥

١٤- ادعوا إلى الله بالعمل الصالح
Supplicate to Allaah through righteous deeds

Narrated Ibn `Umar: The Prophet (ﷺ) said, "While three persons were walking, rain began to fall and they had to enter a cave in a mountain. A big rock rolled over and blocked the mouth of the cave. They said to each other, 'Invoke Allah with the best deed you have performed (so Allaah might remove the rock)'. One of them said, 'O Allaah! My parents were old, and I used to go out for grazing (my animals). On my return I would milk (the animals) and take the milk in a vessel to my parents to drink. After they had drunk from it, I would give it to my children, family and wife. One day I was delayed and on my return, I found my parents sleeping, and I disliked to wake them up. The children were crying at my feet (because of hunger). That state of affairs continued till it was dawn. O Allaah! If You regard that I did it for Your sake, then please remove this rock so that we may see the sky.' So, the rock was moved a bit. The second said, 'O Allaah! You know that I was in love with a cousin of mine, like the deepest love a man may have for a woman, and she told me that I would not get my desire fulfilled unless I paid her one-hundred Dinars (gold pieces). So, I struggled for it till I gathered the desired amount, and when I sat in between her legs, she told me to be afraid of Allah, and asked me not to deflower her except rightfully (by marriage). So, I got up and left her. O Allaah! If You regard that I did if for Your sake, kindly remove this rock.' So, two-thirds of the rock was removed. Then the third man said, 'O Allaah! No doubt You know that once I employed a worker for one Faraq (three Sa's) of millet, and when I wanted to pay him, he refused to take it, so I sowed it and from its yield I bought cows and a shepherd. After a time that man came and demanded his money. I said to him: Go to those cows and the shepherd and take them for they are for you. He asked me whether I was joking with him. I told him that I was not joking with him, and all that belonged to him. O Allaah! If You regard that I did it sincerely for Your sake, then please remove the rock.' So, the rock was removed completely from the mouth of the cave." Al-Bukhari 2215

١٥- ادعوا ثلاث مرات
Supplicate three times

عَنِ ابْنِ مَسْعُودٍ، قَالَ بَيْنَمَا رَسُولُ اللَّهِ صلى الله عليه وسلم يُصَلِّي عِنْدَ الْبَيْتِ وَأَبُو جَهْلٍ وَأَصْحَابٌ لَهُ جُلُوسٌ وَقَدْ نُحِرَتْ جَزُورٌ بِالأَمْسِ فَقَالَ أَبُو جَهْلٍ أَيُّكُمْ يَقُومُ إِلَى سَلَا جَزُورِ بَنِي فُلاَنٍ فَيَأْخُذُهُ فَيَضَعُهُ فِي كَتِفَيْ مُحَمَّدٍ إِذَا سَجَدَ فَانْبَعَثَ أَشْقَى الْقَوْمِ فَأَخَذَهُ فَلَمَّا سَجَدَ النَّبِيُّ صلى الله عليه وسلم وَضَعَهُ بَيْنَ كَتِفَيْهِ قَالَ فَاسْتَضْحَكُوا وَجَعَلَ بَعْضُهُمْ يَمِيلُ عَلَى بَعْضٍ وَأَنَا قَائِمٌ أَنْظُرُ . لَوْ كَانَتْ لِي مَنَعَةٌ طَرَحْتُهُ عَنْ ظَهْرِ رَسُولِ اللَّهِ صلى الله عليه وسلم وَالنَّبِيُّ صلى الله عليه وسلم سَاجِدٌ مَا يَرْفَعُ رَأْسَهُ حَتَّى انْطَلَقَ إِنْسَانٌ فَأَخْبَرَ فَاطِمَةَ فَجَاءَتْ وَهِيَ جُوَيْرِيَةٌ فَطَرَحَتْهُ عَنْهُ . ثُمَّ أَقْبَلَتْ عَلَيْهِمْ تَشْتِمُهُمْ فَلَمَّا قَضَى النَّبِيُّ صلى الله عليه وسلم صَلاَتَهُ رَفَعَ صَوْتَهُ ثُمَّ دَعَا عَلَيْهِمْ وَكَانَ إِذَا دَعَا دَعَا ثَلاَثًا . وَإِذَا سَأَلَ سَأَلَ ثَلاَثًا ثُمَّ قَالَ " اللَّهُمَّ عَلَيْكَ بِقُرَيْشٍ " . ثَلاَثَ مَرَّاتٍ فَلَمَّا سَمِعُوا صَوْتَهُ ذَهَبَ عَنْهُمُ الضِّحْكُ وَخَافُوا دَعْوَتَهُ ثُمَّ قَالَ " اللَّهُمَّ عَلَيْكَ بِأَبِي جَهْلِ بْنِ هِشَامٍ وَعُتْبَةَ بْنِ رَبِيعَةَ وَشَيْبَةَ بْنِ رَبِيعَةَ وَالْوَلِيدِ بْنِ عُقْبَةَ وَأُمَيَّةَ بْنِ خَلَفٍ وَعُقْبَةَ بْنِ أَبِي مُعَيْطٍ " . وَذَكَرَ السَّابِعَ وَلَمْ أَحْفَظْهُ فَوَالَّذِي بَعَثَ مُحَمَّدًا صلى الله عليه وسلم بِالْحَقِّ لَقَدْ رَأَيْتُ الَّذِينَ سَمَّى صَرْعَى يَوْمَ بَدْرٍ ثُمَّ سُحِبُوا إِلَى الْقَلِيبِ قَلِيبِ بَدْرٍ. قَالَ أَبُو إِسْحَاقَ الْوَلِيدُ بْنُ عُقْبَةَ غَلَطٌ فِي هَذَا الْحَدِيثِ . مسلم ١٧٩٤

It has been narrated on the authority of Ibn Mas'ud who said: While the Messenger of Allaah (ﷺ) was saying his prayer near the Ka'ba and Abu Jahl with his companions was sitting (near by), Abu Jahl said. referring to the she-camel that had been slaughtered the previous day: Who will rise to fetch the fetus of the she-camel of so and so, and place it between the shoulders of Muhammad when he goes down in prostration (a posture in prayer). The one most accursed among the people got up, brought the fetus and, when the Prophet (ﷺ) went down in prostration, placed it between his shoulders. Then they laughed at him and some of them leaned upon the others with laughter. And I stood looking. If I had the power, I would have thrown it away from the back of the Messenger of Allaah (ﷺ). The Prophet (ﷺ) had bent down his head in prostration and did not raise it, until a man went (to his house) and informed (his daughter) Fatima, who was a young girl (at that time) (about this ugly incident). She came and removed (the filthy thing) from him. Then she turned towards them rebuking them (the mischief-mongers). When the Prophet (ﷺ) had finished his prayer, he invoked God's imprecations upon them in a loud voice. When he prayed, he prayed thrice, and when he asked for God's blessings, he asked thrice. Then he said thrice: O Allaah, it is for Thee to deal with the Quraish. When they heard his voice, laughter vanished from them and they feared his malediction. Then he said: O God, it is for Thee to deal with Abu Jahl b. Hisham, 'Utba b. Rabi'a, Shaiba b. Rabi'a. Walid b. Uqba, Umayya b. Khalaf, Uqba b. Abu Mu'ait (and he mentioned the name of the seventh person. which I did not remember). By One Who sent Muhammad with truth, I saw (all) those he had named lying slain on the Day of Badr. Their dead bodies were dragged to be thrown into a pit near the battlefield. Abu Ishiq had said that the name of Walid b. 'Uqba has been wrongly mentioned in this tradition. Muslim 1794

١٦- ادعوا نحو القبلة
Pray toward the Qiblah

حَدَّثَنَا يَحْيَى بْنُ يَحْيَى، أَخْبَرَنَا سُلَيْمَانُ بْنُ بِلاَلٍ، عَنْ يَحْيَى بْنِ سَعِيدٍ، قَالَ أَخْبَرَنِي أَبُو بَكْرِ بْنُ مُحَمَّدِ بْنِ عَمْرِو، أَنَّ عَبَّادَ بْنَ تَمِيمٍ، أَخْبَرَهُ أَنَّ عَبْدَ اللَّهِ بْنَ زَيْدٍ الأَنْصَارِيَّ أَخْبَرَهُ أَنَّ رَسُولَ اللَّهِ صلى الله عليه وسلم خَرَجَ إِلَى الْمُصَلَّى يَسْتَسْقِي وَأَنَّهُ لَمَّا أَرَادَ أَنْ يَدْعُوَ اسْتَقْبَلَ الْقِبْلَةَ وَحَوَّلَ رِدَاءَهُ . مسلم ٨٩٤

Abdullah b. Zaid al-Ansari reported that the Messenger of Allaah ﷺ went out to the place of prayer in order to offer prayer for rainfall. And when he intended to make a supplication, he faced Qibla and turned round his mantle. Muslim 894

١٧- ارفعوا يديك عند الدعاء (لكن لا بعد الفرائض لأنه لا يوجد الدليل في السنة على ذلك)
Raise your hands when supplicating, however not after obligatory prayers, as there is no proof for that from the Sunnah.

عَنْ سَلْمَانَ، قَالَ قَالَ رَسُولُ اللَّهِ صلى الله عليه وسلم " إِنَّ رَبَّكُمْ تَبَارَكَ وَتَعَالَى حَيِيٌّ كَرِيمٌ يَسْتَحْيِي مِنْ عَبْدِهِ إِذَا رَفَعَ يَدَيْهِ إِلَيْهِ أَنْ يَرُدَّهُمَا صِفْرًا " . سنن أبي داود ١٤٨٨ حكم: صحيح الألباني

Narrated Salman al-Farsi: The Prophet ﷺ said: Your Lord is munificent and generous, and is ashamed to turn away empty the hands of His servant when he raises them to Him. Sunan Abi Dawud 1488

١٨- توضؤوا قبل الدعاء
Perform wudu before supplicating

عَنْ أَبِي مُوسَى ـ رضى الله عنه ـ قَالَ لَمَّا فَرَغَ النَّبِيُّ صلى الله عليه وسلم مِنْ حُنَيْنٍ بَعَثَ أَبَا عَامِرٍ عَلَى جَيْشٍ إِلَى أَوْطَاسٍ فَلَقِيَ دُرَيْدَ بْنَ الصِّمَّةِ، فَقُتِلَ دُرَيْدٌ وَهَزَمَ اللَّهُ أَصْحَابَهُ. قَالَ أَبُو مُوسَى وَبَعَثَنِي مَعَ أَبِي عَامِرٍ فَرُمِيَ أَبُو عَامِرٍ فِي رُكْبَتِهِ، رَمَاهُ جُشَمِيٌّ بِسَهْمٍ فَأَثْبَتَهُ فِي رُكْبَتِهِ، فَانْتَهَيْتُ إِلَيْهِ فَقُلْتُ يَا عَمِّ مَنْ رَمَاكَ فَأَشَارَ إِلَى أَبِي مُوسَى فَقَالَ ذَاكَ قَاتِلِي الَّذِي رَمَانِي. فَقَصَدْتُ لَهُ فَلَحِقْتُهُ فَلَمَّا رَآنِي وَلَّى فَاتَّبَعْتُهُ وَجَعَلْتُ أَقُولُ لَهُ أَلاَ تَسْتَحِي، أَلاَ تَثْبُتْ. فَكَفَّ فَاخْتَلَفْنَا ضَرْبَتَيْنِ بِالسَّيْفِ فَقَتَلْتُهُ ثُمَّ قُلْتُ لأَبِي عَامِرٍ قَتَلَ اللَّهُ صَاحِبَكَ. قَالَ فَانْزِعْ هَذَا السَّهْمَ فَنَزَعْتُهُ فَنَزَا مِنْهُ الْمَاءُ. قَالَ يَا ابْنَ أَخِي أَقْرِئِ النَّبِيَّ صلى الله عليه وسلم السَّلاَمَ، وَقُلْ لَهُ اسْتَغْفِرْ لِي. وَاسْتَخْلَفَنِي أَبُو عَامِرٍ عَلَى النَّاسِ، فَمَكَثَ يَسِيرًا ثُمَّ مَاتَ، فَرَجَعْتُ فَدَخَلْتُ عَلَى النَّبِيِّ صلى الله عليه وسلم فِي بَيْتِهِ عَلَى سَرِيرٍ مُرْمَلٍ وَعَلَيْهِ فِرَاشٌ قَدْ أَثَّرَ رِمَالُ السَّرِيرِ بِظَهْرِهِ وَجَنْبَيْهِ، فَأَخْبَرْتُهُ بِخَبَرِنَا وَخَبَرِ أَبِي عَامِرٍ، وَقَالَ قُلْ لَهُ اسْتَغْفِرْ لِي، فَدَعَا بِمَاءٍ فَتَوَضَّأَ ثُمَّ رَفَعَ يَدَيْهِ فَقَالَ " اللَّهُمَّ اغْفِرْ لِعُبَيْدٍ أَبِي عَامِرٍ ". وَرَأَيْتُ بَيَاضَ إِبْطَيْهِ ثُمَّ قَالَ " اللَّهُمَّ اجْعَلْهُ يَوْمَ الْقِيَامَةِ فَوْقَ كَثِيرٍ مِنْ خَلْقِكَ مِنَ النَّاسِ, . فَقُلْتُ وَلِي فَاسْتَغْفِرْ. فَقَالَ " اللَّهُمَّ اغْفِرْ لِعَبْدِ اللَّهِ بْنِ قَيْسٍ ذَنْبَهُ وَأَدْخِلْهُ يَوْمَ الْقِيَامَةِ مُدْخَلاً كَرِيمًا "
قَالَ أَبُو بُرْدَةَ إِحْدَاهُمَا لأَبِي عَامِرٍ وَالأُخْرَى لأَبِي مُوسَى. البخاري ٤٣٢٣

Narrated Abu Musa: When the Prophet ﷺ had finished from the battle of Hunain, he sent Abu Amir at the head of an army to Autas He (i.e. Abu Amir) met Duraid bin As Summa and Duraid was killed and Allaah defeated his companions. The Prophet ﷺ sent me with Abu 'Amir. Abu Amir was shot at his knee with an arrow which a man from Jushm had shot and fixed into his knee. I went to him and said, "O Uncle! Who shot you?" He pointed me out (his killer) saying, "That is my killer who shot me (with an arrow)." So I headed towards him and overtook him, and when he saw me, he fled, and I followed him and started saying to him, "Won't you be ashamed? Won't you stop?" So that person stopped, and we exchanged two hits with the swords, and I killed him. Then I said to Abu 'Amir. "Allaah has killed your killer." He said, "Take out this arrow" So I removed it, and water oozed out of the wound. He then said, "O son of my brother! Convey my compliments to the Prophet ﷺ and request him to ask Allah's Forgiveness for me." Abu Amir made me his successor in commanding the people (i.e. troops). He survived for a short while and then died. (Later) I returned and entered upon the Prophet ﷺ at his house and found him lying in a bed made of stalks of date-palm leaves knitted with ropes, and on it there was bedding. The strings of the bed had their traces over his back and sides. Then I told the Prophet ﷺ about our and Abu Amir's news and how he had said "Tell him to ask for Allaah's Forgiveness for me." The Prophet ﷺ asked for water, performed ablution and then raised hands, saying, "O Allaah's Forgive `Ubaid, Abu Amir." At that time I saw the whiteness of the Prophet's armpits. The Prophet ﷺ then said, "O Allaah, make him (i.e. Abu Amir) on the Day of Resurrection, superior to many of Your human creatures." I said, "Will you ask Allah's Forgiveness for me?" (On that) the Prophet ﷺ said, "O Allaah, forgive the sins of `Abdullah bin Qais and admit him to a nice entrance (i.e. paradise) on the Day of Resurrection." Abu Burda said, "One of the prayers was for Abu 'Amir and the other was for Abu Musa (i.e. `Abdullah bin Qais). Bukhari 4323

١٩- ابكوا أثناء الدعاء
Weep while supplicating

عَنْ عَبْدِ اللَّهِ بْنِ عَمْرِو بْنِ الْعَاصِ، أَنَّ النَّبِيَّ صلى الله عليه وسلم تَلاَ قَوْلَ اللَّهِ عَزَّ وَجَلَّ فِي إِبْرَاهِيمَ { رَبِّ إِنَّهُنَّ أَضْلَلْنَ كَثِيرًا مِنَ النَّاسِ فَمَنْ تَبِعَنِي فَإِنَّهُ مِنِّي} الآيَةَ . وَقَالَ عِيسَى عَلَيْهِ السَّلاَمُ { إِنْ تُعَذِّبْهُمْ فَإِنَّهُمْ عِبَادُكَ وَإِنْ تَغْفِرْ لَهُمْ فَإِنَّكَ أَنْتَ الْعَزِيزُ الْحَكِيمُ} فَرَفَعَ يَدَيْهِ وَقَالَ " اللَّهُمَّ أُمَّتِي أُمَّتِي " . وَبَكَى فَقَالَ اللَّهُ عَزَّ وَجَلَّ يَا جِبْرِيلُ اذْهَبْ إِلَى مُحَمَّدٍ وَرَبُّكَ أَعْلَمُ فَسَلْهُ مَا يُبْكِيكَ فَأَتَاهُ جِبْرِيلُ - عَلَيْهِ الصَّلاَةُ وَالسَّلاَمُ - فَسَأَلَهُ فَأَخْبَرَهُ رَسُولُ اللَّهِ صلى الله عليه وسلم بِمَا قَالَ . وَهُوَ أَعْلَمُ . فَقَالَ اللَّهُ يَا جِبْرِيلُ اذْهَبْ إِلَى مُحَمَّدٍ فَقُلْ إِنَّا سَنُرْضِيكَ فِي أُمَّتِكَ وَلاَ نَسُوءُكَ . مسلم ٢٠٢

Abdullah b. Amr b. al-'As reported: Verily the Messenger of Allaah ﷺ recited the words of Allaah, the Great and Glorious, that Ibrahim uttered. My Lord, they have led many people astray. Whoever follows me belongs with me; and whoever disobeys me–You are Forgiving and Merciful. (Ibrahim: 36) and Isa (peace be upon him) said:" If You punish them, they are Your servants; but if You forgive them, You are the Mighty and Wise." (Maidah: 118). Then he ﷺ raised his hands and said: O Lord, my Ummah, my Ummah, and wept; so Allaah the High and the Exalted said: O Jibreel, go to Muhammad (though your Lord knows it fully well) and ask him: What makes you weep? So Gabriel (peace be upon him) came to him and asked him, and the Messenger of Allaah ﷺ informed him what he had said (though Allaah knew it fully well). Upon this Allaah said: O Jibreel, go to Muhammad and say: Verily, We will please you with regard to your Ummah and would not displease you. Muslim 202

٢٠- يجب عليك أن تظهر كلامك الحاجة والعوز والفقر أمام الله وكذلك توجيه شكواك إلى الله تعالى الضعف والانقباض والتجارب التي تواجهها.

You must display your utter need, destitution, and poverty before Allaah, as well as directing your complaint to Allaah due to weakness, constriction, and trials you encounter.

﴿وَأَيُّوبَ إِذْ نَادَى رَبَّهُ أَنِّي مَسَّنِيَ الضُّرُّ وَأَنْتَ أَرْحَمُ الرَّاحِمِينَ﴾ الأنبياء ٨٣

And Ayyub, when he cried out to his Lord: "Great harm has afflicted me, and you are the Most Merciful of the merciful." Al-Anbiya: 83

٢١- ابدأ بدعاء من أجل أنفسك قبل الآخرين
Begin with supplicating for yourself before others

عَنِ ابْنِ عَبَّاسٍ، عَنْ أُبَيِّ بْنِ كَعْبٍ، أَنَّ رَسُولَ اللَّهِ صلى الله عليه وسلم كَانَ إِذَا ذَكَرَ أَحَدًا فَدَعَا لَهُ بَدَأَ بِنَفْسِهِ . الترمذي ٣٣٨٥ حكم: حسن

Ibn `Abbas narrated from Ubayy bin Ka`b that: whenever the Messenger of Allaah ﷺ would mention someone and supplicate for him, he would begin with himself ﷺ.

٢٢- لا تتعدوا/تتجاوزوا في الدعاء
Do not transgress in supplication

عَنِ ابْنِ لِسَعْدٍ، أَنَّهُ قَالَ سَمِعَنِي أَبِي، وَأَنَا أَقُولُ اللَّهُمَّ، إِنِّي أَسْأَلُكَ الْجَنَّةَ وَنَعِيمَهَا وَبَهْجَتَهَا وَكَذَا وَكَذَا وَأَعُوذُ بِكَ مِنَ النَّارِ وَسَلَاسِلِهَا وَأَغْلَالِهَا وَكَذَا وَكَذَا فَقَالَ يَا بُنَيَّ إِنِّي سَمِعْتُ رَسُولَ اللَّهِ صلى الله عليه وسلم يَقُولُ " سَيَكُونُ قَوْمٌ يَعْتَدُونَ فِي الدُّعَاءِ " . فَإِيَّاكَ أَنْ تَكُونَ مِنْهُمْ إِنْ أُعْطِيتَ الْجَنَّةَ أُعْطِيتَهَا وَمَا فِيهَا مِنَ الْخَيْرِ وَإِنْ أُعِذْتَ مِنَ النَّارِ أُعِذْتَ مِنْهَا وَمَا فِيهَا مِنَ الشَّرِّ . سنن أبي داود ١٤٠ حكم: صحيح الألباني

Narrated Sa'd ibn Abu Waqqas: Ibn Sa'd said: My father (Sa'd ibn Abu Waqqas) heard me say: O Allaah, I ask Thee for Paradise, its blessings, its pleasure and such-and-such, and such-and-such; I seek refuge in Thee from Hell, from its chains, from its collars, and from such-and-such, and from such-and-such. He said: I heard the Messenger of Allaah ﷺ say: There will be people who will exaggerate in supplication. You should not be one of them. If you are granted Paradise, you will be granted all what is good therein; if you are protected from Hell, you will be protected from what is evil therein. Sunan Abi Dawud 140

NOTES:

NOTES:

NOTES:

الأوقات والظروف والأماكن التي تستجاب الدعاء

Times, Circumstances and Places Supplications are Answered

Laylatul Qadr (Refer to the Surah & Tafseer)

The last third of the night: Narrated Abu Huraira: Allaah's Messenger ﷺ said, "Our Lord, the Blessed, the Superior, comes every night down on the nearest Heaven to us when the last third of the night remains, saying: "Is there anyone to invoke Me, so that I may respond to invocation? Is there anyone to ask Me, so that I may grant him his request? Is there anyone seeking My forgiveness, so that I may forgive him?" Bukhari 1145 Jabir reported: I heard the Messenger of Allaah ﷺ as saying: There is an hour during the night in which no Muslim bondman will ask Allah for good in this world and the next, but He will grant it to him. Muslim 757

Between the Adhan and the Iqaamah: Anas bin Malik narrated that Allah's Messenger ﷺ said: "The supplication made between the Adhan and Iqaamah is not rejected." Tirmidhi 212 Graded Sahih Ibn Hibban

During prayer, the closet that a slave is to his Lord is when he is in a state of prostration: Abu Huraira reported: The Messenger of Allah ﷺ said: The nearest a servant comes to his Lord is when he is prostrating himself, so make supplication (in this state). Muslim 482

Before the end of the prayer after the tashahhud: Malik said: There is no harm in uttering supplication in prayer, in its beginning, in its middle, and in the end, in obligatory prayer or other. Sunan Abi Dawud 769 Graded Sahih Maqtu' Al-Albani: Abdullah said: "I was praying, and the Prophet, Abu Bakr, and Umar were there, so when I sat, I started off with praising Allah, then sending Salat upon the Prophet, then supplicating for myself. So the Prophet said: 'Ask, your request will be granted, ask, your request will be granted.'"
At-Tirmidhi 593 Graded Sahih

After the prayer, after you've finished your adhkar.

An hour on Friday or a period of time on Friday; the scholars differ over when this is. Some of them said that is when the Imam sits down between the two Khutbah, and some say it is at the last period of time before Maghrib. Nevertheless frequently making dua on Friday during the two times previously mentioned, after the khutbah and then just before Maghrib in shaa Allaah they will be accepted

During rainfall: "Seek the response to your supplications when the armies meet, and the prayer is called, and when rain falls." (Reported by Imam al-Shafi' in al-Umm) The time of the rain is a time of mercy from Allaah سبحانه وتعالى so, one should take advantage of this time when Allah is having mercy on His slaves.

While drinking ZamZam water with sincere intention: It was narrated that Jabir bin 'Abdullah said: "I heard the Messenger of Allaah ﷺ say: 'The water of Zamzam is for whatever it is drunk for.'" Sunan Ibn Majah 3062 Graded Hasan: This means that when you drink Zamzam water you may ask Allaah سبحانه وتعالى for anything you like to gain or benefit from this water such as healing from illness.... etc.

When sleeping after having been in a state of purity, then awaking in the night and supplicating: It was narrated from Mu'adh bin Jabal that the Messenger of Allaah ﷺ said: "There is no person who goes to bed in a state of purity, then wakes up at night, and asks Allaah for something in this world or the Hereafter, but it will be given to him." Sunan Ibn Majah 3881 Graded Hasan

While saying the dua of Prophet Yunus "لا إله إلا أنت سبحانك إني كنت من الظالمين" (There is none worthy of worship except you, glory be to You, verily I am from the wrong doers). Ibrahim bin Muhammad bin Sa`d narrated from his father, from Sa`d that the Messenger of Allaah ﷺ said: "The supplication of Dhun-Nun (Prophet Yunus) when he supplicated, while in the belly of the whale was: 'There is none worthy of worship except You, Glory to You, Indeed, I have been of the transgressors. (La ilāha illa anta subḥanaka innī kuntu minaẓ-ẓalimīn)' So indeed, no Muslim man supplicates with it for anything, ever, except Allaah responds to him." At-Tirmidhi 3505 Graded Sahih Shaykh Al-Albani

The supplication of the oppressed against those who oppress him: Ibn 'Abbas narrated: "The Messenger of Allaah (ﷺ) sent Mu'adh [bin Jabal] to Yemen and said: 'Beware of the supplication of the oppressed; for indeed there is no barrier between it and Allah.'" At-Tirmidhi 2014 Graded Sahih

The Traveler/The supplication of a parent for their child: It was narrated that Abu Hurairah reported that the Messenger of Allaah ﷺ said: "There are three supplications that will undoubtedly be answered: the supplication of one who has been wronged; the supplication of the traveler; and the supplication of a father for his child." Sunan Ibn Majah 3862

The sincere and heartfelt supplication of a Muslim for his (Muslim) brother in his absence: Abu Dharr reported that Allaah's Messenger ﷺ said: There is no believing servant who supplicates for his brother behind his back (in his absence) that the Angels do not say: The same be for you too. Muslim 2732a

Day of Arafat

While marching in a military formation in the cause of Allaah : Narrated Sahl ibn Sa'd: The Prophet ﷺ said: Two (prayers) are not rejected, or seldom rejected: Prayer at the time of the call to prayer, and (the prayer) at the time of fighting, when the people grapple with each other. Sunan Abi Dawud 2540 Graded Sahih Shaykh Al-Albani When the Muslim is facing the enemy in battle, at this critical period, the du'a of a worshiper is accepted.

First 10 days of Dhul-Hijja: Narrated Ibn `Abbas: The Prophet ﷺ said, "No good deeds done on other days are superior to those done on these (first ten days of Dhul-Hijja)." Then some companions of the Prophet ﷺ said, "Not even Jihad?" He replied, "Not even Jihad, except that of a man who does it by putting himself and his property in danger (for Allaah's sake) and does not return with any of those things. Sahih Bukhari 969

Dua of the one fasting until he breaks his fast/dua of the one fasting at the time of breaking fast & supplication of a just ruler: It was narrated that Abu Hurairah said: The Messenger of Allaah (ﷺ) said: "There are three whose du'a are not rejected: a just ruler, the fasting person when he breaks his fast and the prayer of the oppressed person. It rises above the clouds and the gates of heaven are opened for it, and the Lord, may He be glorified, says, 'By My Glory I will answer you even if it is after a while.'" Narrated by al-Tirmidhi, 2525; classed as Sahih by al-Albaani in Saheeh al-Tirmidhi, 2050; In another narration, the fasting person until he breaks his fast.

Dua of a son or daughter obedient to his or her parents: While mentioning the etiquettes of supplicating, we came across the hadeeth in Bukhari 2215 ,in which in the story narrated in hadith of the three men who were trapped by a huge stone in a cave. One of them, who was kind to his parents, asked Allah to remove the stone, and his du'a was answered.

Dua of a son or daughter obedient to his or her parents: While mentioning the etiquettes of supplicating, we came across the hadeeth in Bukhari 2215, in which in the story narrated in hadith of the three men who were trapped by a huge stone in a cave. One of them who was kind to his parents, asked Allah to remove the stone, and his du'a was answered.

The supplication offered directly after wudu.

The supplications that can happen at various times during Hajj, as well as various in Saudi (Ka'bah, Safa & Marwa etc.)

NOTES:

NOTES:

NOTES:

Supplication 1: Upon Seeing the Crescent Moon

عَنْ ابْنِ عُمَرَ رَضِيَ اللهِ عَنْهُ قَالَ كَانَ رَسُولُ اللَّهِ صَلَّى اللَّهُ عَلَيْهِ وَسَلَّمَ إِذَا رَأَى الْهِلَالَ قَالَ اللَّهُ أَكْبَرُ اللَّهُمَّ أَهِلَّهُ عَلَيْنَا بِالْأَمْنِ وَالْإِيمَانِ وَالسَّلَامَةِ وَالْإِسْلَامِ وَالتَّوْفِيقِ لِمَا يُحِبُّ رَبُّنَا وَيَرْضَى رَبُّنَا وَرَبُّكَ اللَّهُ

صحيح لغيره في تخريج صحيح ابن حبان ٨٨٨

Ibn Umar reported: Whenever the Messenger of Allaah (ﷺ), saw the new crescent moon, he would say, "Allaah is the greatest! O Allaah, bring it over us with safety and faith, peace and Islam, and guidance to what our Lord loves and is pleased with. Our Lord and your Lord is Allaah."

Arabic

اللَّهُ أَكْبَرُ اللَّهُمَّ أَهِلَّهُ عَلَيْنَا بِالْأَمْنِ وَالْإِيمَانِ وَالسَّلَامَةِ وَالْإِسْلَامِ وَالتَّوْفِيقِ لِمَا يُحِبُّ رَبُّنَا وَيَرْضَى رَبُّنَا وَرَبُّكَ اللَّهُ

Transliteration

Allaahu Akbar, Allaahumma A-Hilla-who alane na Bil-am-ne, wal-imaanee Was-Salaama-te Wal-Islaame, Wat-Tawfeeqi Li Maa You-Hib-Bu Rabblrub)-bun-naa Wa Yar-Daa Rab-bu-naa Wa Rabbukallahu

Word-by-Word

And the success	وَالتَّوْفِيقِ	Allaah is The Greatest	اللَّهُ أَكْبَرُ
To what he loves	لِمَا يُحِبُّ	Oh Allaah	اللَّهُمَّ
Our Lord	رَبُّنَا	Bring it	أَهِلَّهُ
And what he is pleased with	وَيَرْضَى	Over us	عَلَيْنَا
Our Lord & Your Lord is	رَبُّنَا وَرَبُّكَ	With Safety & Faith	بِالْأَمْنِ وَالْإِيمَانِ
Allaah	اللَّهُ	And Peace & Islaam	وَالسَّلَامَةِ وَالْإِسْلَامِ

NOTES:

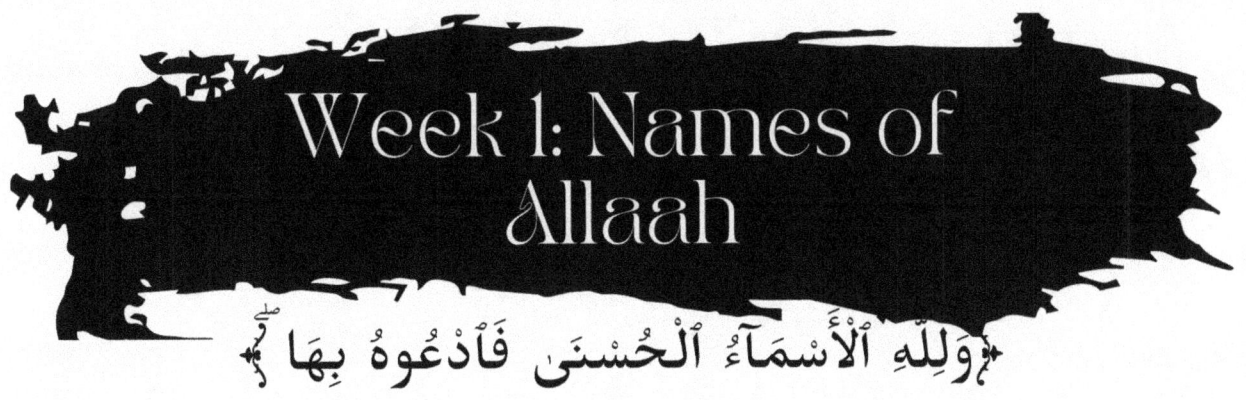

Week 1: Names of Allaah

﴿وَلِلَّهِ ٱلْأَسْمَآءُ ٱلْحُسْنَىٰ فَٱدْعُوهُ بِهَا﴾

"Allaah has the Most Beautiful Names. So call upon Him by them" A'raaf: 180

Allaah

الرَّبُّ

Ar-Rabb: The Lord

الرَّحْمٰنُ

**Ar-Rahmaan
The Most Merciful**

43

NOTES:

NOTES:

NOTES:

الرَّحِيمُ
Ar-Raheem
The Bestower of Mercy

الْحَيُّ
Al-Hayy
The Ever-living

الْقَيُّومُ
Al-Qayyoom
The Self-Subsisting Sustainer

الْخَالِقُ
Al Khaaliq
The Creator

NOTES:

NOTES:

NOTES:

الْخَلَّاق

Al-Khallaq
The Ever Creating

الْبَارِئ

Al-Baari
The Originator

الْمُصَوِّر

Al-Musawwir
The Fashioner of Forms

NOTES:

NOTES:

NOTES:

اَلْمَلِك
Al-Malik
The King

الْمَلِيك
Al-Maleek
The Supreme Sovereign

الرَّزَّاق
Ar-Razzaaq
The Great Provider

الرَّازِق
Ar-Raaziq
The Best of Sustainers

NOTES:

NOTES:

NOTES:

الأَحَد
Al-Ahad
The Unique

الوَاحِد
Al-Waahid
The One

الصَّمَد
As-Samad
The Self-Sufficient Master

الهَادِي
Al-Haadee
The Guide

NOTES:

NOTES:

NOTES:

الوهاب
Al-Wahhaab
The Bestower

الفتاح
Al-Fattaah
The Just Judge

السميع
As-Samee'
The All-Hearer

البصير
Al-Baseer
The All-Seer

NOTES:

NOTES:

NOTES:

```
W  Z  J  U  J  L  A  E  O  H  D  E
A  R  V  X  L  Q  A  L  K  F  J  L
R  A  W  U  F  X  C  L  L  E  U  X
R  L  P  Q  T  Y  A  I  H  A  J  C
A  K  A  L  B  A  A  R  I  A  A  K
H  H  A  L  M  A  L  E  E  K  Y  H
E  A  L  N  A  L  M  A  L  I  K  Y
E  A  A  L  M  U  S  A  W  W  I  R
M  L  A  L  Q  A  Y  Y  O  O  M  X
I  I  D  A  R  R  A  H  M  A  A  N
P  Q  A  L  K  H  A  L  L  A  A  Q
K  U  P  A  R  R  A  B  B  I  C  B
```

Allaah	Ar Rabb	Ar Rahmaan	Ar Raheem
Al Hayy	Al Qayyoom	Al Khaaliq	Al Khallaaq
Al Baari	Al Musawwir	Al Malik	Al Maleek

Unscramble the following names of Allah.

| Al Musawwir | Ar Rahmaan | Al Malik | Ar Raheem | Al Khallaaq | Ar Rabb |
| Al Baari | Allaah | Al Maleek | Al Hayy | Al Qayyoom | Al Khaaliq |

1. AALLHA _____

2. RA BBAR _____

3. RA ARNMHAA _____

4. RA EEHMRA _____

5. LA AYHY _____

6. LA MOYOQYA _____

7. LA AIAHKLQ _____

8. LA QAALKHAL _____

9. LA RBAAI _____

10. LA RWAIMWUS _____

11. LA AMKLI _____

12. LA MELEKA _____

Self-reflection is an essential part of preparing for Ramadhaan.

Umar ibn Al-Khattaab, may Allaah be pleased with him, said: "Call yourselves to account before you are called to account, and weigh yourselves before you are weighed, as calling yourselves to account today will make it easier for you when you are called to account tomorrow, and be adorned for the great appearance: that Day shall you be brought to Judgment, not a secret of you will be hidden."

Al-Hasan Al-Basri may Allaah be pleased with him, said: "The true believer is a guardian of his own self and continuously calls his soul to account for the sake of Allaah. The reckoning of the Day of Resurrection will only be easy for those who continuously call their souls to account in the life of this world. The reckoning of the Day of Resurrection will only be difficult for those who live the life of this world without ever examining their conscience and calling themselves to account."

And Allaah says in Suratul Hashr: 18-19

يَٰٓأَيُّهَا ٱلَّذِينَ ءَامَنُوا۟ ٱتَّقُوا۟ ٱللَّهَ وَلْتَنظُرْ نَفْسٌ مَّا قَدَّمَتْ لِغَدٍ ۖ وَٱتَّقُوا۟ ٱللَّهَ ۚ إِنَّ ٱللَّهَ خَبِيرٌۢ بِمَا تَعْمَلُونَ, وَلَا تَكُونُوا۟ كَٱلَّذِينَ نَسُوا۟ ٱللَّهَ فَأَنسَىٰهُمْ أَنفُسَهُمْ ۚ أُو۟لَٰٓئِكَ هُمُ ٱلْفَٰسِقُونَ

O you who have believed, fear Allāah. And let every soul look to what it has put forth for tomorrow - and fear Allāah. Indeed, Allāah is Aware of what you do. And be not like those who forgot Allāah, so He made them forget themselves. Those are the defiantly disobedient.

And Allaah says in Suratuz-Zumar: 54

وَأَنِيبُوٓا۟ إِلَىٰ رَبِّكُمْ وَأَسْلِمُوا۟ لَهُۥ مِن قَبْلِ أَن يَأْتِيَكُمُ ٱلْعَذَابُ ثُمَّ لَا تُنصَرُونَ

And return [in repentance] to your Lord and submit to Him before the punishment comes upon you; then you will not be helped.

Reflecting on your actions, intentions, and relationships allows you to realign with your faith and build a stronger connection with Allaah.

Utilize this section to journal and reflect on ways to strengthen your relationship with Allaah and develope and maintain healthy habits on your journey to rectify your affairs before you are called to account for them.

May Allaah, Al-Wahhabb, bestow upon us the ability to be from those who remain in a state of muhasabah (constantly evaluating one's actions and behavior of the nafs; and then rectifying mistakes and continuing upon good). May Allaah only call our souls in a state which he is pleased with us and give us a good ending Aameen

Reflecting on Your Spiritual & Personal Growth

Reconnect with Your Faith

Directions for Weekly Reflections: Each week consists of a prompt for spiritual and personal growth.

- Week 1: Focus on Prompt 1: **Spiritual** - What steps can I take to strengthen my relationship with Allaah before, during, and after Ramadhaan? **Personal** - What personal habits do I want to leave behind or improve during Ramadhaan?
    - Reflect deeply on this question and write actionable steps in the space provided.
    - Track your progress throughout the week using the progress tracker.
    - Reflect on traits such as patience, self-discipline, or gratitude.
    - Write specific habits you'd like to focus on changing.

Reflecting on Your Spiritual & Personal Growth

Reconnect with Your Faith

Directions for Weekly Reflections: Each week consists of a prompt for spiritual and personal growth.

- Week 2: Focus on Prompt 2: **Spiritual** - Which area of my worship needs the most improvement? **Personal** - How can I use fasting to develop greater self-discipline and self-control?
    - Identify one area of worship to improve and write down specific actions to implement this week.
    - Reflect on moments during fasting when you may struggle and how to overcome those challenges.
    - Write down practical strategies to practice patience and mindfulness while fasting.

Progress Tracker

Week 1: Strengthen Relationship with Allaah

Week 2: Improve Area of Worship

Reflecting on Your Spiritual & Personal Growth

Reconnect with Your Faith

Directions for Weekly Reflections: Each week consists of a prompt for spiritual and personal growth.

- Week 3: Focus on Prompt 3: **Spiritual** - What specific supplications do I want to consistently make this Ramadhaan? **Personal** - What worldly distractions can I reduce or eliminate to focus more on worship?
    - Create a list of key supplications and start memorizing or incorporating them into your daily routine.
    - Identify activities (e.g., excessive screen time, unnecessary socializing) that pull you away from worship.
    - Write down steps to minimize or replace these distractions with beneficial activities.

Reflecting on Your Spiritual & Personal Growth

Reconnect with Your Faith

Directions for Weekly Reflections: Each week consists of a prompt for spiritual and personal growth.

- Week 4: Focus on Prompt 4: **Spiritual** - How can I ensure I stay consistent in my spiritual goals even after Ramadhaan ends? **Personal** - How can I use Ramadhaan to improve my relationships with family and friends?
    - Reflect on habits and create a sustainable post-Ramadhaan plan.
    - Reflect on ways to connect, forgive, or spend quality time with loved ones.
    - Write down actions to improve these relationships, such as sharing Iftars or performing acts of kindness.

Progress Tracker

Week 3: Focus on Personal Habits

Week 4: Focus on Supplications

Reflecting on Your Spiritual & Personal Growth

Reconnect with Your Faith

Directions for Weekly Reflections: Each week consists of a prompt for spiritual and personal growth.

- Week 5: Focus on Prompt 5: **Spiritual** - Am I dedicating enough time to understanding and reflecting on the Qur'an? **Personal** - What daily habits can I build this month to carry on after Ramadhaan ends?
    - Write a list of habits you want to build (e.g., daily dhikr, Qur'aan recitation, consistent salah).
    - Set a daily Qur'aan reflection routine and document your progress.
    - Think of ways to integrate these habits into your routine beyond Ramadhaan.

_____
_____
_____
_____
_____
_____
_____
_____
_____
_____
_____
_____
_____
_____
_____
_____

Reflecting on Your Spiritual & Personal Growth

Reconnect with Your Faith

Directions for Weekly Reflections: Each week consists of a prompt for spiritual and personal growth.

- Week 6: Focus on Prompt 6: **Spiritual** - What distractions prevent me from fully connecting with Allah, and how can I minimize them? **Personal** - How do I handle challenges or setbacks during fasting, and how can I improve my response?
    - List distractions and actionable strategies to minimize or eliminate them.
    - Reflect on past difficulties (e.g., irritability, fatigue) and how you can address them this year.
    - Write specific strategies to stay calm and focused, such as breathing exercises or seeking support through dua.

Progress Tracker

Week 5: Consistency in Spiritual & Personal Goals

Week 6: Minimize Distractions

Take time to pause and reflect on your answers. Use these reflections to guide your goals and create a meaningful Ramadhaan experience.

Remember, progress over perfection! Focus on growth and consistency In Shaa Allaah.

عَنْ عَائِشَةَ، أَنَّ رَسُولَ اللَّهِ صلى الله عليه وسلم قَالَ " سَدِّدُوا وَقَارِبُوا، وَاعْلَمُوا أَنْ لَنْ يُدْخِلَ أَحَدَكُمْ عَمَلُهُ الْجَنَّةَ، وَأَنَّ أَحَبَّ الأَعْمَالِ أَدْوَمُهَا إِلَى اللَّهِ، وَإِنْ قَلَّ "

Narrated `Aisha (May Allaah be pleased with her):
Allaah's Messenger (ﷺ) said, "Do good deeds properly, sincerely and moderately and know that your deeds will not make you enter Paradise, and that the most beloved deed to Allaah is the most regular and constant even if it were little."
(Sahih al-Bukhari 6464)

And Allaah says in Suratur-Ra'd: 11

إِنَّ ٱللَّهَ لَا يُغَيِّرُ مَا بِقَوْمٍ حَتَّىٰ يُغَيِّرُوا۟ مَا بِأَنفُسِهِمْ

Allaah will not change the condition of a people until they change what is in themselves.

May Allaah grant you success in your journey and the ability to maintain consistent deeds and acts of worship! Aameen

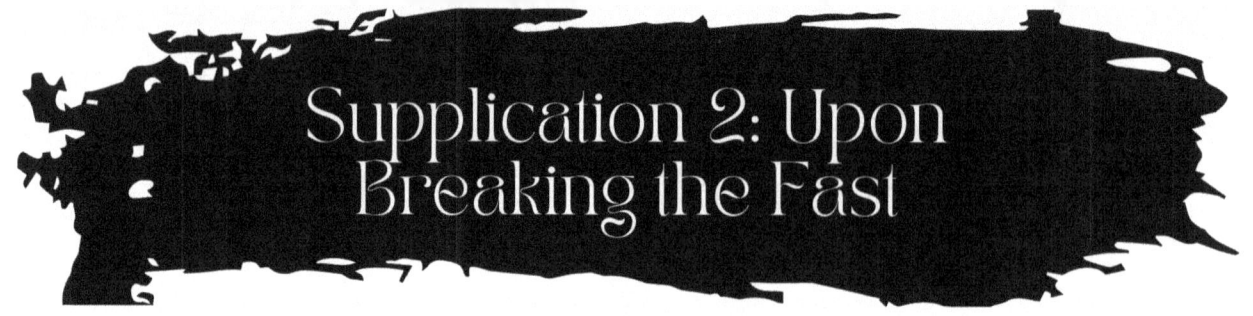

Supplication 2: Upon Breaking the Fast

حَدَّثَنَا مَرْوَانُ، - يَعْنِي ابْنَ سَالِمٍ - الْمُقَفَّعُ - قَالَ رَأَيْتُ ابْنَ عُمَرَ يَقْبِضُ عَلَى لِحْيَتِهِ فَيَقْطَعُ مَا زَادَ عَلَى الْكَفِّ وَقَالَ كَانَ رَسُولُ اللَّهِ صلى الله عليه وسلم إِذَا أَفْطَرَ قَالَ " ذَهَبَ الظَّمَأُ وَابْتَلَّتِ الْعُرُوقُ وَثَبَتَ الأَجْرُ إِنْ شَاءَ اللَّهُ "

Marwan ibn Salim al-Muqaffa' said: I saw Ibn Umar holding his beard with his hand and cutting what exceeded the handful of said when he broke ﷺ it. He (Ibn Umar) said that the Prophet his fast: Thirst has gone, the arteries are moist, and the reward is sure, if Allah wills. Sunan Abi Dawud 2357

Arabic

ذَهَبَ الظَّمَأُ وَابْتَلَّتِ الْعُرُوقُ وَثَبَتَ الأَجْرُ إِنْ شَاءَ اللَّهُ

Transliteration

Thahabadh-dhama'u wabtallatil-'urooqu, Wa tha batal 'ajru 'inshaa'Allah.

Word-by-Word

ذَهَبَ	To Go/Gone	وَثَبَتَ	Confirmed/Established
الظَّمَأُ	The thirst	الأَجْرُ	Reward
وَابْتَلَّتِ	Moistened	إِنْ شَاءَ اللَّهُ	If Allaah Wills
الْعُرُوقُ	Veins		

NOTES:

Week 2: Names of Allaah

الْعَلِيمُ

Al-Aleem
The All-Knowing

اللَّطِيفُ

Al-Lateef
The Subtle & Kind

الْخَبِيرُ

Al-Khabeer
The Fully Aware

NOTES:

NOTES:

NOTES:

الْعَفْوُ
Al-Afwu
The Pardoner

الْغَفُورُ
Al-Ghafoor
The Ever-Forgiving

الْعَلِيُّ
Al-Alee
The Exalted

NOTES:

NOTES:

NOTES:

الْأَعْلَى
Al-A'laa
The Most High

الْمُتَعَالِي
Al-Muta'aal
The Supreme & Exalted One

الْكَبِيرُ
Al-Kabeer
The Most Great

الْعَظِيمُ
Al-'Adheem
The Magnificent

NOTES:

NOTES:

NOTES:

القوي
Al-Qawee
The One Perfect in Strength

المتين
Al-Mateen
The Strong

الشهيد
Ash-Shaheed
The Witness

NOTES:

NOTES:

NOTES:

الرَّقِيب
Ar-Raheem
The Bestower of Mercy

الْمُهَيْمِن
Al-Muhaymin
The Ever-Watchful Witness

الْمُحِيط
A;-Muheet
The All-Encompassing

الْمُقِيت
Al-Muqeet
The All-Powerful Maintainer & Guardian

NOTES:

NOTES:

NOTES:

الْوَاسِع
Al-Waasi'
The Vast One

الْحَفِيظُ
Al-Haafeedh
The Guardian &
Preserver

الْحَافِظ
Al-Haafidh
The Protector

NOTES:

NOTES:

NOTES:

Across
1. The Great Provider
2. The Unique
5. The Guide
7. The All Seeing
8. The All Knowing
12. The Fully Aware

Dow
1. The Subtle and Kind
3. The One
4. The Self Sufficient Master
6. The Bestower
7. The Just Judge
8. The All Hearing

Names of Allaah - Week 2

1	☐	Ar-Razzaaq	The All Seeing	A
2	☐	Al-Ahad	The All Hearing	B
3	☐	Al-Waahid	The One	C
4	☐	As-Samad	The Just Judge	D
5	☐	Al-Haadee	The All Knowing	E
6	☐	Al-Wahhaab	The Self Sufficient Master	F
7	☐	Al-Fattaah	The Subtle and Kind	G
8	☐	As-Samee'	The Unique	H
9	☐	Al-Baseer	The Great Provider	I
10	☐	Al 'Aleem	The Bestower	J
11	☐	Al-Lateef	The Guide	K
12	☐	Al-Khabeer	The Fully Aware	L

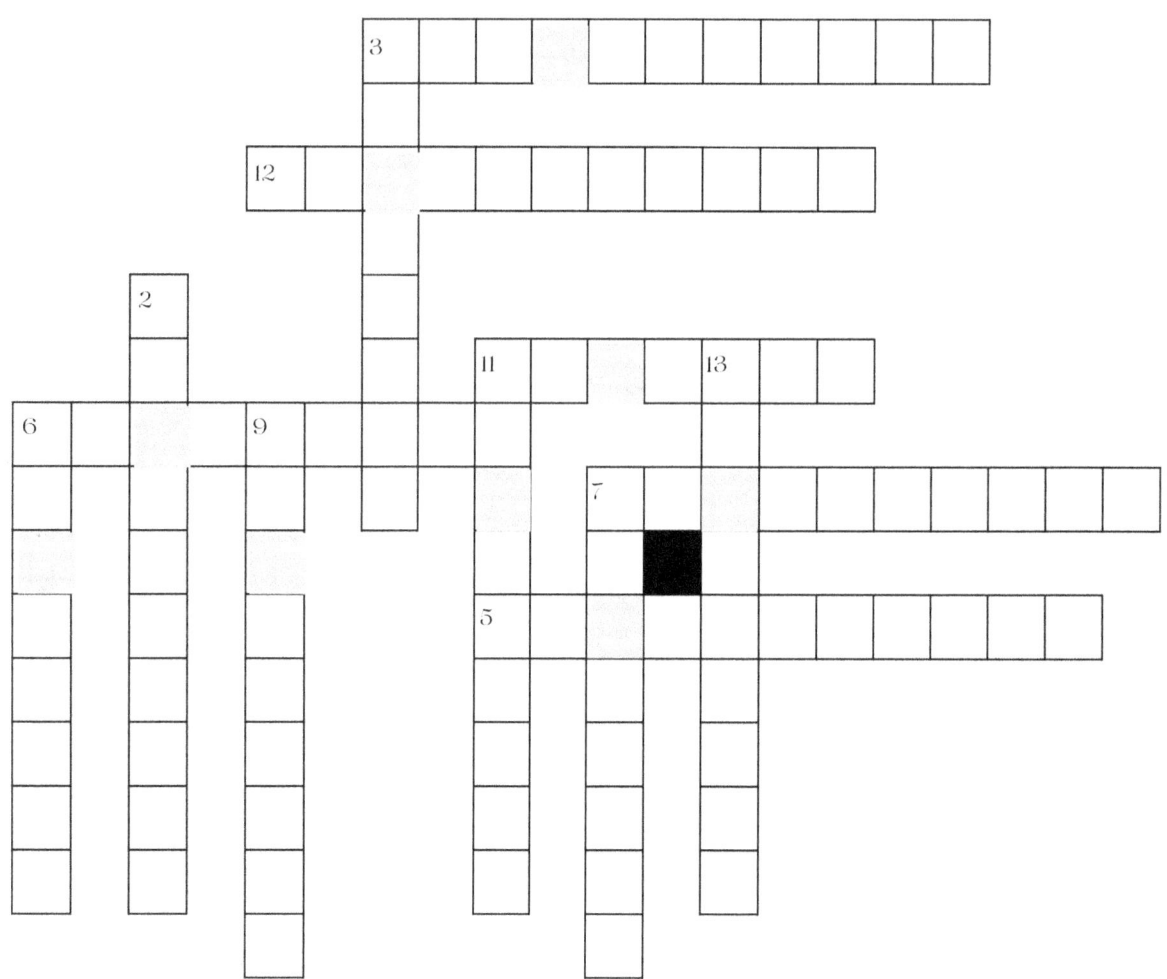

Across
3. The Witness
5. The Supreme and Exalted One
6. The Most Great
7. The Magnificient
11. The Pardoner
12. The Ever Watchful Witness

Dow
12. The Ever Forgiving
3. The Exalted
6. The Most High
7. The One Perfect in Strength
9. The Strong
11. The Ever Watchful Guardian
13. The All Encompassing

Al A'laa	Al Qawee	Al Muhaymin	Al 'Adheem	Al Kabeer	Al Muta'aal
Al Mateen	Al Ghafoor	Al Muheet	Ar Raqeeb	Al 'Afw	Ash Shaheed
Al 'Alee					

1. LA F'WA _ _ _ _ _ _

2. LA OAORGFH _ _ _ _ _ _ _ _

3. LA AEL'E _ _ _ _ _ _

4. LA 'AALA _ _ _ _ _ _

5. LA ALAAT'MU _ _ _ _ _ _ _ _ _

6. LA AKREEB _ _ _ _ _ _ _

7. LA 'HMADEE _ _ _ _ _ _ _ _

8. LA WEQEA _ _ _ _ _ _ _

9. LA TNMEEA _ _ _ _ _ _ _

10. SAH AHHEESD _ _ _ _ _ _ _ _ _

11. RA QREEBA _ _ _ _ _ _ _

12. LA MAUYNMIH _ _ _ _ _ _ _ _ _

13. LA EUHEMT _ _ _ _ _ _ _

Intentions & Goal Setting

Intentions are the foundation of every action! Setting intentions is one of the most powerful aspects of preparing for Ramadhaan.

By focusing on our intentions, we align our hearts and minds with our worship, ensuring that even the smallest acts carry great spiritual value.

Intentions act as the foundation for our goals. Without clear intentions, our efforts can lose focus. Setting an intention is like planting a seed; nurturing it through consistent actions and mindfulness allows it to flourish.

عن عُمَرَ بْنِ الْخَطَّابِ، يَقُولُ قَالَ رَسُولُ اللَّهِ صلى الله عليه وسلم" إِنَّمَا الأَعْمَالُ بِالنِّيَّاتِ وَإِنَّمَا لِكُلِّ امْرِئٍ مَا نَوَى فَمَنْ كَانَتْ هِجْرَتُهُ إِلَى اللَّهِ وَرَسُولِهِ فَهِجْرَتُهُ إِلَى اللَّهِ وَرَسُولِهِ وَمَنْ كَانَتْ هِجْرَتُهُ لِدُنْيَا يُصِيبُهَا أَوِ امْرَأَةٍ يَتَزَوَّجُهَا فَهِجْرَتُهُ إِلَى مَا هَاجَرَ إِلَيْهِ "

Narrated 'Umar bin Al Khattab (May Allaah be pleased with him) reported the Messenger of Allaah ﷺ as saying "Actions are but by intentions, and each man will have but that which he intended. Whoever emigrated for the sake of Allaah and His Messenger, his emigration was for the sake of Allaah and His Messenger, and whoever emigrated for the sake of some worldly gain or to marry some woman, his emigration was for that for which he emigrated."
(Sahih al-Bukhari 1)

During Ramadhaan, this practice becomes even more significant as our deeds carry multiplied rewards. Therefore, take the time to reflect deeply on your purpose for fasting, worship, and personal growth.

Introduction to SMART Goals Framework:

Why Use SMART Goals for Ramadhaan? During Ramadhaan, it's easy to get overwhelmed with the desire to maximize worship, improve personal habits, and contribute to the community. The SMART framework helps you focus on attainable objectives while maintaining balance. By setting clear, structured goals, you ensure that your efforts are meaningful, sustainable, and aligned with the essence of this blessed month.

How to Apply SMART Goals:
- Reflect on your spiritual, personal, and community aspirations for Ramadhaan.
- Use the SMART framework to define these aspirations into clear, actionable goals.
- Break down larger goals into smaller steps for daily or weekly progress.
- Regularly review your progress and adjust as needed to stay aligned with your intentions.

By incorporating SMART goals into your Ramadhaan preparation, you not only enhance your focus and productivity, but also ensure that your journey through the month is purposeful and fulfilling.

SMART Goals Framework:

Use the SMART framework to make your goals Specific, Measurable, Achievable, Relevant, and Time-bound.

- Specific: Clearly define what you want to achieve (e.g., "I will recite one page of the Qur'aan daily").
- Measurable: Track progress (e.g., "I will mark off each day I recite the Qur'aan in my tracker").
- Achievable: Set goals within your capacity (e.g., "I will memorize one dua each week rather than multiple at once").
- Relevant: Align goals with your spiritual purpose (e.g., "I will focus on dhikr to strengthen my connection with Allah").
- Time-bound: Attach a time frame to your goals (e.g., "Complete my Qur'an reading schedule by the 29th of Ramadhaan").

Make Them Specific and Measurable:
- Instead of "I want to be a better Muslim," reframe it as "I will pray all five daily prayers on time." Specific intentions are easier to track and fulfill.

Focus on Quality, Not Quantity:
- A few meaningful goals are better than overwhelming yourself with too many.

Tie Your Intentions to Worship:
- For example, "I intend to strengthen my relationship with Allaah by completing one Juz of the Qur'aan daily."

Review and Renew Regularly:
- Revisit your intentions weekly to ensure you're staying on track and make adjustments as needed.

By grounding your goals in intentionality, you create a framework that not only prepares you for Ramadhaan, but also helps you sustain spiritual growth long after the blessed month has ended.

Use the following section to set clear goals and intentions for Ramadhaan.

SETTING SMART GOALS

Example Goal: Memorizing the Qunoot

Specific — What do I want to accomplish and why? I want to memorize the Qunoot so that I am able to understand it when it is recited and I am able to recite it when I am praying Tahajjud Taraweeh alone.

Measurable — How will I know when I have accomplished it? When I am able to recite the Qunoot with ease and full understanding of each word.

Achievable — How can I accomplish this goal? Every day after Dhur, I will take one sentence from the qunoot, break down each word, memorize the words by writing and saying them repeatedly. I will also listen to an audio to help with memorization.

Relevant — Is this the right time for me to be working towards this goal? With Ramadhaan approaching this is perfect timing to memorize this supplication and I will manage my time wisely to complete my goal.

Timebound — When do I want to accomplish this goal by? I would like to accomplish this goal within 15 days in shaa Allaah.

Goal:

Specific — What do I want to accomplish and why?

Measurable — How will I know when I have accomplished it?

Achievable — How can I accomplish this goal?

Relevant — Is this the right time for me to be working towards this goal?

Timebound — When do I want to accomplish this goal by?

Goal:

Specific — What do I want to accomplish and why?

Measurable — How will I know when I have accomplished it?

Achievable — How can I accomplish this goal?

Relevant — Is this the right time for me to be working towards this goal?

Timebound — When do I want to accomplish this goal by?

Goal:

Specific — What do I want to accomplish and why?

Measurable — How will I know when I have accomplished it?

Achievable — How can I accomplish this goal?

Relevant — Is this the right time for me to be working towards this goal?

Timebound — When do I want to accomplish this goal by?

Goal:

Specific – What do I want to accomplish and why?

Measurable – How will I know when I have accomplished it?

Achievable – How can I accomplish this goal?

Relevant – Is this the right time for me to be working towards this goal?

Timebound – When do I want to accomplish this goal by?

Goal:

Specific – What do I want to accomplish and why?

Measurable – How will I know when I have accomplished it?

Achievable – How can I accomplish this goal?

Relevant – Is this the right time for me to be working towards this goal?

Timebound – When do I want to accomplish this goal by?

Goal:

Specific — What do I want to accomplish and why?

Measurable — How will I know when I have accomplished it?

Achievable — How can I accomplish this goal?

Relevant — Is this the right time for me to be working towards this goal?

Timebound — When do I want to accomplish this goal by?

Goal:

Specific — What do I want to accomplish and why?

Measurable — How will I know when I have accomplished it?

Achievable — How can I accomplish this goal?

Relevant — Is this the right time for me to be working towards this goal?

Timebound — When do I want to accomplish this goal by?

Goal:

Specific – What do I want to accomplish and why?

Measurable – How will I know when I have accomplished it?

Achievable – How can I accomplish this goal?

Relevant – Is this the right time for me to be working towards this goal?

Timebound – When do I want to accomplish this goal by?

Goal:

Specific – What do I want to accomplish and why?

Measurable – How will I know when I have accomplished it?

Achievable – How can I accomplish this goal?

Relevant – Is this the right time for me to be working towards this goal?

Timebound – When do I want to accomplish this goal by?

Goal:

Specific — What do I want to accomplish and why?

Measurable — How will I know when I have accomplished it?

Achievable — How can I accomplish this goal?

Relevant — Is this the right time for me to be working towards this goal?

Timebound — When do I want to accomplish this goal by?

Goal:

Specific — What do I want to accomplish and why?

Measurable — How will I know when I have accomplished it?

Achievable — How can I accomplish this goal?

Relevant — Is this the right time for me to be working towards this goal?

Timebound — When do I want to accomplish this goal by?

SPIRITUAL GOALS

GOALS	ACTION PLAN	PURPOSE

PERSONAL GOALS

GOALS	ACTION PLAN	PURPOSE

Week 3

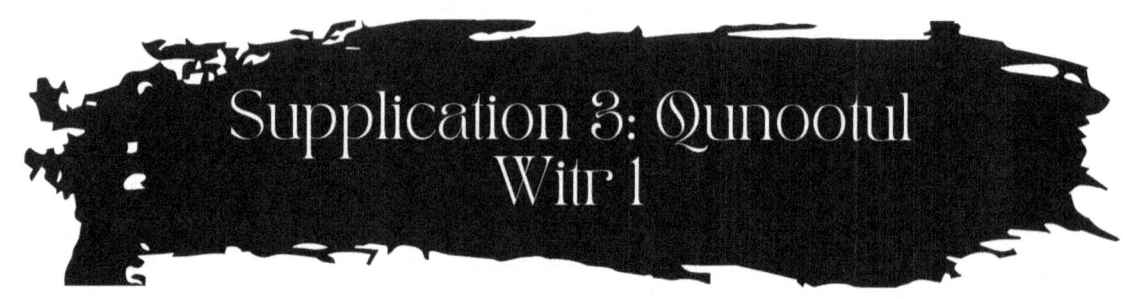

Supplication 3: Qunootul Witr 1

قَالَ الْحَسَنُ بْنُ عَلِيٍّ رضى الله عنهما عَلَّمَنِي رَسُولُ اللَّهِ صلى الله عليه وسلم كَلِمَاتٍ أَقُولُهُنَّ فِي الْوِتْرِ قَالَ ابْنُ جَوَّاسٍ فِي قُنُوتِ الْوِتْرِ " اللَّهُمَّ اهْدِنِي فِيمَنْ هَدَيْتَ وَعَافِنِي فِيمَنْ عَافَيْتَ وَتَوَلَّنِي فِيمَنْ تَوَلَّيْتَ وَبَارِكْ لِي فِيمَا أَعْطَيْتَ وَقِنِي شَرَّ مَا قَضَيْتَ إِنَّكَ تَقْضِي وَلاَ يُقْضَى عَلَيْكَ وَإِنَّهُ لاَ يَذِلُّ مَنْ وَالَيْتَ وَلاَ يَعِزُّ مَنْ عَادَيْتَ تَبَارَكْتَ رَبَّنَا وَتَعَالَيْتَ "

Al-Hasan Ibn 'Alee (May Allaah be pleased with him) said: Allaah's Messenger ﷺ taught me some words to say during the Qunoot of the Witr prayer
O Allaah, guide me with those You have guided, heal me with those You have healed, care for me as a companion with those You have cared for, bless me in what You have given and protect me from the evil of what You have decreed. Indeed, You decree while no one decrees against You. Whomever You show loyalty towards will never be humiliated, and whoever You show enmity towards will never be honored. Blessed are You, our Lord, and You are exalted far above (any deficiencies)." Sunan Abi Dawud 1425

Arabic

اللَّهُمَّ اهْدِنِي فِيمَنْ هَدَيْتَ وَعَافِنِي فِيمَنْ عَافَيْتَ وَتَوَلَّنِي فِيمَنْ تَوَلَّيْتَ وَبَارِكْ لِي فِيمَا أَعْطَيْتَ

Transliteration

Allaahum-mahdinee feeman hadayta, wa 'aafinee feeman 'aafayta, wa tawallanee feeman tawallayta, wa baarik lee feemaa 'a'atayta

Supplication 3: Qunoot Witr 1

Word-by-Word

O Allaah	اللَّهُمَّ	Care for me	وَتَوَلَّنِي
Guide me	اهْدِنِي	With those	فِيمَنْ
With those	فِيمَنْ	You have cared for	تَوَلَّيْتَ
You have guided	هَدَيْتَ	And bless me	وَبَارِكْ لِي
Heal me	وَعَافِنِي	In what	فِيمَا
With those	فِيمَنْ	You have given	أَعْطَيْتَ
You have healed	عَافَيْتَ		

NOTES:

Week 3: Names of Allaah

"Allaah has the Most Beautiful Names. So call upon Him by them" A'raaf: 180

الوَلِيُّ
Al-Walee
The Protector

الْمَوْلَى
Al-Mawlaa
The Protector & Supporter

NOTES:

NOTES:

NOTES:

الأوَّلُ
**Al-Awwal
The First**

الآخِرُ
**Al-Aakhir
The Last**

الظَّاهِرُ
**Adh-Dhaahir
The Uppermost**

الباطِنُ
**Al-Baatin
The Closet**

NOTES:

NOTES:

NOTES:

Al-Hakeem
The All-Wise

Al-Ghanee
The Rich Free of All Need

Al-Kareem
The Generous

NOTES:

NOTES:

NOTES:

الأَكْرَم
Al-Akram
The Most Generous

السَّلام
As-Salaam
The One Free From all Defects

القُدُّوس
Al-Quddoos
The Pure & Perfect

NOTES:

NOTES:

NOTES:

السُّبُّوح
As-Subbooh
The Supremelt Glorious

الحميد
Al-Hameed
The Praiseworthy

المجيد
Al-Majeed
The One Perfect in Glory & Honor

الشكور
Ash-Shakoor
The Most Ready to Appreciate and Reward Abundatly

NOTES:

NOTES:

NOTES:

الشَّاكِر
Ash-Shaakir
The Appreciative

الحَلِيم
Al-Haleem
The Forebearing

الحَقّ
Al-Haqq
The True One

المُبِين
Al-Mubeen
The Clear &
Manifest One

NOTES:

NOTES:

NOTES:

#	Name	Meaning	
1	Al Muqeet	The Uppermost	A
2	Al Waasi'	The Protector	B
3	Al Hafeedth	The Last	C
4	Al Haafidh	The Closest One	D
5	Al Walee	The First	E
6	Al Mawlaa	The All Wise	F
7	Al Awwal	The Guardian and Preserver	G
8	Al Aakhir	The All Powerful Maintainer and Guardian	H
9	Adh Dhaahir	The Protector	I
10	Al Baatin	The Vast One	J
11	Al Hakeem	The Protector and Supporter	K
12	Al Ghanee	The Rich Free of All Need	L

```
U N W E Z A L W A L E E
Z A L H A K E E M Q F A
F A L H A A F I D H A L
G W A L W A A S I ' V H
H A L M U Q E E T N M A
A A D H D H A A H I R F
L A L A A K H I R K M E
A A Q Q N V S B B P T E
W N B A S G E I Y O Q D
W A L M A W L A A M B T
A A L G H A N E E W J H
L A L B A A T I N M W T
```

Al Muqeet   Al Waasi'   Al Hafeedth   Al Haafidh
Al Walee   Al Mawlaa   Al Awwal   Al Aakhir
Adh Dhaahir   Al Baatin   Al Hakeem   Al Ghanee

Practical Tips for Fasting Preparation

Introduction

Fasting during Ramadhaan is a divine obligation and a profound spiritual practice. Allaah says in the Qur'aan:

يَٰٓأَيُّهَا ٱلَّذِينَ ءَامَنُوا۟ كُتِبَ عَلَيْكُمُ ٱلصِّيَامُ كَمَا كُتِبَ عَلَى ٱلَّذِينَ مِن قَبْلِكُمْ لَعَلَّكُمْ تَتَّقُونَ

O you who have believed, decreed upon you is fasting as it was decreed upon those before you that you may become righteous [Baqarah: 183]

This verse highlights the primary goal of fasting: attaining taqwa (God-consciousness). The physical act of fasting goes hand in hand with mental and spiritual preparation, ensuring that you make the most of this blessed month.

Prophet Muhammad (ﷺ) also emphasized the rewards of fasting, saying:

عَنْ أَبِي هُرَيْرَةَ، قَالَ قَالَ رَسُولُ اللَّهِ صلى الله عليه وسلم " مَنْ صَامَ رَمَضَانَ إِيمَانًا وَاحْتِسَابًا غُفِرَ لَهُ مَا تَقَدَّمَ مِنْ ذَنْبِهِ ".

Abu Huraira narrated: Allaah's Messenger (ﷺ) said, "Whoever observes fasts during the month of Ramadan out of sincere faith, and hoping to attain Allah's rewards, then all his past sins will be forgiven." Bukhari 38

To maximize the benefits of fasting, it is essential to prepare both physically and mentally.

Adjusting Sleep Routines

Plan for Suhoor: Suhoor, the pre-dawn meal, is a Sunnah of the Prophet (ﷺ), it is mentioned in a hadeeth narrated by Anas Ibn Maalik:

أَنَسَ بْنَ مَالِكٍ ـ رضى الله عنه ـ قَالَ قَالَ النَّبِيُّ صلى الله عليه وسلم " تَسَحَّرُوا فَإِنَّ فِي السَّحُورِ بَرَكَةً ."

The Prophet (ﷺ) said, "Eat Suhoor, for in Suhoor there is blessing."

Begin adjusting your sleep schedule a week before Ramadhaan to wake up early for Suhoor.

Prioritize Rest: Ensure you get sufficient rest at night and consider power naps during the day to maintain energy levels.

Avoid Oversleeping: Oversleeping can make you lethargic and reduce the time available for worship and other acts of devotion.

Dietary Preparation

Eat Moderately: Follow the advice of the Prophet (ﷺ):

الْمِقْدَامَ بْنَ مَعْدِيكَرِبَ، يَقُولُ سَمِعْتُ رَسُولَ اللَّهِ ـ صلى الله عليه وسلم ـ يَقُولُ " مَا مَلأَ آدَمِيٌّ وِعَاءً شَرًّا مِنْ بَطْنٍ حَسْبُ الآدَمِيِّ لُقَيْمَاتٌ يُقِمْنَ صُلْبَهُ فَإِنْ غَلَبَتِ الآدَمِيَّ نَفْسُهُ فَثُلُثٌ لِلطَّعَامِ وَثُلُثٌ لِلشَّرَابِ وَثُلُثٌ لِلنَّفَسِ " .

Miqdam bin Madikarib (May Allaah be please with him) said: "I heard the Messenger of Allaah (ﷺ) say: 'A human being fills no worse vessel than his stomach. It is sufficient for a human being to eat a few mouthfuls to keep his spine straight. But if he must (fill it), then one third of food, one third for drink and one third for air.'"

Incorporate Sunnah Foods: Include dates in your meals, as the Prophet (peace be upon him) used to break his fast with dates:

عَنْ أَنَسِ بْنِ مَالِكٍ، يَقُولُ كَانَ رَسُولُ اللَّهِ صلى الله عليه وسلم يُفْطِرُ عَلَى رُطَبَاتٍ قَبْلَ أَنْ يُصَلِّيَ فَإِنْ لَمْ تَكُنْ رُطَبَاتٌ فَعَلَى تَمَرَاتٍ فَإِنْ لَمْ تَكُنْ حَسَا حَسَوَاتٍ مِنْ مَاءٍ .

Narrated Anas ibn Malik (May Allaah be pleased with him): The Messenger of Allaah (ﷺ) used to break his fast before praying with some fresh dates; but if there were no fresh dates, he had a few dry dates, and if there were no dry dates, he took some mouthfuls of water. Sunan Abi Dawud 2356

Reduce Caffeine and Sugary Drinks: Gradually cut back on coffee, tea, and sugary beverages to avoid withdrawal symptoms during fasting.

Stay Hydrated: Drink plenty of water between Iftar and Suhoor to prevent dehydration.

Sunnah Foods

Consider incorporating these foods into your Suhoor and Iftar for a wholesome, Sunnah-inspired diet:

Olives & Figs: Mentioned in the Qur'an as a blessed food (Surah At-Tin, 95:1).

Honey: The Prophet (peace be upon him) recommended honey for its healing properties (Sahih al-Bukhari 5688).

Milk: The Prophet (peace be upon him) frequently consumed milk as part of his meals (Sunan Ibn Majah 3324).

Barley: Often used in traditional recipes like Talbina, barley was highly valued in the Prophet's time (Sunan Ibn Majah 3442).

Pomegranate: Mentioned in the Qur'aan as one of the fruits of Paradise (Surah Al-An'aam, 6:99).

Watermelon: The Prophet (peace be upon him) enjoyed watermelon paired with dates

Dates & Cucumbers: (Sunan Ibn Majah 3325)

Mental & Physical Preparation

Develop Focus through Dhikr: Begin incorporating regular dhikr into your day, such as saying SubhanAllah, Alhamdulillah, and Allahu Akbar 100 times each. Constantly seek forgiveness throughout the day. Be sure to do the morning and evening supplications. This practice prepares your mind for increased spirituality during Ramadhaan.

Limit Distractions: Reduce unnecessary screen time or socializing that does not contribute to your spiritual goals.

Set Intentions for Worship: Reflect on your intentions and write them down, focusing on sincerity and seeking Allaah's pleasure.

Gradual Transition to Fasting: If you are not used to fasting, try fasting a few days before Ramadhaan, such as on Mondays and Thursdays, following the Sunnah of the Prophet (peace be upon him).

Exercise Wisely: Engage in light physical activities such as walking or stretching to maintain energy without overexertion.

Organize Your Environment: Clean and prepare your home, especially your prayer area, to create a conducive environment for worship.

Plan Your Meals: To make the most of your time and avoid the hassle of deciding what to prepare for Suhoor or Iftar, plan your meals in advance. Additionally, try to do your grocery shopping early in the morning to avoid going when you are extremely hungry, which can lead to impulsive choices.

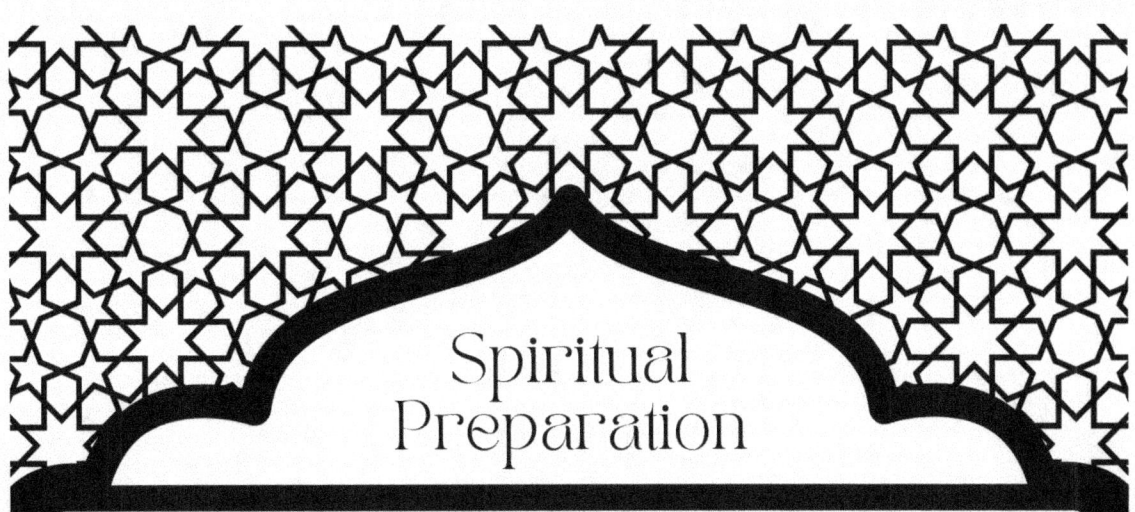

Spiritual Preparation

Renewing Your Intentions: Reflect on your purpose for fasting and performing acts of worship. Allaah says: "And they were not commanded except to worship Allaah, [being] sincere to Him in religion, inclining to truth..." (Surah Al-Bayyinah, 98:5)
Write down your intentions, whether it's improving your salah, increasing Qur'aan recitation, or giving more in charity.

Salah Consistency: Prioritize praying all five daily prayers on time, and add Sunnah prayers to your routine. Begin incorporating Tahajjud, even if just two raka'ahs, to deepen your spiritual connection.
Allaah says: "Indeed, prayer prohibits immorality and wrongdoing, and the remembrance of Allaah is greater." (Surah Al-Ankabut, 29:45)

Increase Qur'aan Recitation/Daily Qur'aan Connection: Make a plan to read, understand, and reflect on the Qur'aan daily. Even a few verses a day can make a significant difference.
The Prophet (ﷺ) said:
"The best among you are those who learn the Qur'aan and teach it." (Sahih al-Bukhari 5027)

Spiritual Preparation

Dhikr and Dua: Engage in regular remembrance of Allah throughout the day. The Prophet (ﷺ) said:
"The similitude of the one who remembers his Lord and the one who does not remember Him is like that of the living and the dead." (Sahih al-Bukhari, 6407)

Create a list of supplications to memorize and recite during Suhoor, Iftar, and Laylatul Qadr. Include personal supplications to ask for forgiveness, guidance, and blessings.

Charity and Generosity: Plan acts of kindness and giving during Ramadhaan. The Prophet (peace be upon him) was described as the most generous during this month:
"The Prophet (ﷺ) was the most generous of all the people, and he used to reach the peak of generosity in the month of Ramadhaan..." (Sahih al-Bukhari, 6)
Set aside a portion of your income for Sadaqah and Zakat al-Fitr.

Spiritual Environment Preparation: Create a designated prayer area at home, and ensure it is clean and free from distractions.

Community Connection: Plan to attend Taraweeh prayers at the masjid and participate in community Iftars.
Seek out opportunities to help organize charity drives or teach others about the blessings of Ramadhaan. Start planning acts of charity, such as donating to those in need or volunteering at your local masjid.

Checklists

weekly *checklist* month: week:

tasks: mon tue wed thu fri sat sun

- Begin waking up earlier for Suhoor
- Establish a consistent bedtime to ensure adequate rest
- Gradually reduce caffeine intake to avoid withdrawal symptoms
- Incorporate Sunnah foods into your meals (e.g., dates, olives, honey)
- Plan balanced Suhoor and Iftar meals with a mix of protein, vegetables, and grains
- Stock up on healthy snacks and hydrating foods for Suhoor
- Avoid heavy, fried, or sugary foods to prevent sluggishness
- Reduce screen time and unnecessary distractions
- Write down intentions for worship and personal growth
- Practice daily dhikr to build mindfulness and focus
- Reflect on previous Ramadhaan to identify areas for improvement
- Gradually ease into fasting by observing voluntary fasts (e.g., Mondays and Thursdays)
- Engage in light physical activity (e.g., stretching, walking) to maintain energy
- Organize your home and prayer area for a peaceful worship environment
- Create a Qur'aan reading schedule (e.g., 1 Juz daily) and print a tracker
- Memorize key supplications for Suhoor, Iftar, and Laylatul Qadr
- Plan acts of Sadaqah (e.g., donations, meal distributions)
- Plan to attend Taraweeh prayers or create a routine for praying at home
- Discuss Ramadhaan goals and routines with family members

weekly *checklist*   month: week:

tasks:

	mon	tue	wed	thu	fri	sat	sun
Schedule family Iftars and plan for collective worship activities							
Organize or participate in community service projects (e.g., food drives)							
Help children or younger siblings understand the significance of Ramadhaan							
Complete grocery shopping for Suhoor and Iftar essentials early to avoid crowds							
Prepare meal plans for the first week of Ramadhaan to save time							
Purchase Islamic books or materials for additional learning during the month							

weekly *checklist*   month: week:

tasks: mon tue wed thu fri sat sun

weekly /*checklist*   month: week:

tasks: mon tue wed thu fri sat sun

weekly *checklist*   month: week:

tasks: mon tue wed thu fri sat sun

weekly *checklist*   month: week:

tasks:

	mon	tue	wed	thu	fri	sat	sun

- Begin waking up earlier for Suhoor
- Establish a consistent bedtime to ensure adequate rest
- Gradually reduce caffeine intake to avoid withdrawal symptoms
- Incorporate Sunnah foods into your meals (e.g., dates, olives, honey)
- Plan balanced Suhoor and Iftar meals with a mix of protein, vegetables, and grains
- Stock up on healthy snacks and hydrating foods for Suhoor
- Avoid heavy, fried, or sugary foods to prevent sluggishness
- Reduce screen time and unnecessary distractions
- Write down intentions for worship and personal growth
- Practice daily dhikr to build mindfulness and focus
- Reflect on previous Ramadhaan to identify areas for improvement
- Gradually ease into fasting by observing voluntary fasts (e.g., Mondays and Thursdays)
- Engage in light physical activity (e.g., stretching, walking) to maintain energy
- Organize your home and prayer area for a peaceful worship environment
- Create a Qur'aan reading schedule (e.g., 1 Juz daily) and print a tracker
- Memorize key supplications for Suhoor, Iftar, and Laylatul Qadr
- Plan acts of Sadaqah (e.g., donations, meal distributions)
- Plan to attend Taraweeh prayers or create a routine for praying at home
- Discuss Ramadhaan goals and routines with family members

weekly *checklist*   month: week:

tasks: mon tue wed thu fri sat sun

- Schedule family Iftars and plan for collective worship activities
- Organize or participate in community service projects (e.g., food drives)
- Help children or younger siblings understand the significance of Ramadhaan
- Complete grocery shopping for Suhoor and Iftar essentials early to avoid crowds
- Prepare meal plans for the first week of Ramadhaan to save time
- Purchase Islamic books or materials for additional learning during the month

weekly *checklist* month: week:

tasks:

mon tue wed thu fri sat sun

weekly *checklist* month: week:

tasks: mon tue wed thu fri sat sun

weekly *checklist* month: week:

tasks:

mon tue wed thu fri sat sun

Supplication 4: Qunootul Witr 2

Arabic

وَقِنِي شَرَّ مَا قَضَيْتَ فَإِنَّكَ تَقْضِي وَلاَ يُقْضَى عَلَيْكَ وَإِنَّهُ لاَ يَذِلُّ مَنْ وَالَيْتَ وَلاَ يَعِزُّ مَنْ عَادَيْتَ تَبَارَكْتَ رَبَّنَا وَتَعَالَيْتَ

Transliteration

Wa qinee sharra maa qadhayta, fa'innaka taqdhee wa laa yuqdhaa 'alayka, wa innahu laa yadhillu man wa layt, wa laa ya'izzu man 'aadayt, Tabārakta rabbanā wa ta'āalayt

Word-by-Word

And Protect me	وَقِنِي	Surely, He is	وَإِنَّهُ
Evil	شَرَّ	Not humiliated	لاَ يَذِلُّ
From what you have decreed	مَا قَضَيْتَ	Whom you have befriended	مَنْ وَالَيْتَ
Indeed You	فَإِنَّكَ	And he is not honored	وَلاَ يَعِزُّ
You decree	تَقْضِي	Who you've shown enmity	مَنْ عَادَيْتَ
And no one decrees	وَلاَ يُقْضَى	Blessed you are	تَبَارَكْتَ
Against you	عَلَيْكَ	Our Lord	رَبَّنَا
		You are exalted	وَتَعَالَيْتَ

NOTES:

Week 4: Names of Allaah

الْقَدِير
Al-Qadeer
The All-Powerful

الْقَادِرُ
Al-Qaadir
The Fully Able

الْمُقْتَدِرُ
Al-Muqtadir
The All-Capable

NOTES:

NOTES:

NOTES:

الودود
Al-Wadood
The Loving & The Beloved

البرّ
Al-Barr
The Most Benign & Kind

الرؤوف
Ar-Ra'oof
The Compassionate & Kind

الحسيب
Al-Haseeb
The Reckoner Who Suffices

NOTES:

NOTES:

NOTES:

الْكَافِي
Al-Kaafee
The Sufficient

الْكَفِيل
Al-Kafeel
The Witness

الْوَكِيل
Al-Wakeel
The Guardian -
Disposer of Affairs

الْغَالِب
Al-Ghaalib
The Predominant

النَّصِير
An-Naseer
The Helper

العَزِيزُ
Al-Azeez
The Almighty

الجَبَّارُ
Al-Jabbar
The Exalted &
Almighty
Compeller

NOTES:

NOTES:

NOTES:

Al Qaadir	Al Jabbaar	Ar Ra'oof	Al Azeez	Al Wadood	Al Kafeel
Al Ghaalib	Al Barr	Al Qadeer	An Naseer	Al Haseeb	Al Muqtadir
Al Wakeel					

1. LA EAQERD   _____

2. LA QIRADA   _____

3. LA TIMRUDAQ   _____

4. LA DOAODW   _____

5. LA RARB   _____

6. RA 'ROOFA   _____

7. LA BEASEH   _____

8. LA ALEKEF   _____

9. LA EEAWLK   _____

10. LA BAGHAIL   _____

11. NA RAEESN   _____

12. LA ZEEZA   _____

13. LA RJABAAB   _____

```
C K Y C P A S M T G N A
C A L J A B B A A R Q N
A A A L A Z E E Z M I N
L L L L A L B A R R E A
H W M W Q R K V E H N S
A A U L A A R A R E U E
S D Q H G K D A F X I E
E O T W E X E E ' E E R
E O A L K K O E E O E G
B D D T S P O R L R O L
Y L I A L Q A A D I R F
T I R A L G H A A L I B
```

Al Qadeer   Al Qaadir   Al Muqtadir   Al Wadood   Al Barr
Ar Ra'oof   Al Haseeb   Al Kafeel   Al Wakeel   Al Ghaalib
An Naseer   Al Azeez   Al Jabbaar

#	Name	Meaning	
1	☐ Al Kareem	The Forbearing	A
2	☐ Al Akram	The Pure and Perfect	B
3	☐ As Salaam	The Generous	C
4	☐ Al Quddoos	The Supremely Glorious	D
5	☐ As Subbooh	The Appreciative	E
6	☐ Al Hameed	The One From from All	F
7	☐ Al Majeed	Defects The True One	G
8	☐ Ash Shakoor	The One Most Ready to Appreciate and Reward Abundantly	H
9	☐ Ash Shaakir	The Clear and Manifest One	I
10	☐ Al Haleem	The Praiseworthy	J
11	☐ Al Haqq	The Most Generous	K
12	☐ Al Mubeen	The One Perfect in Glory and Honour	L

Across

2. The Most Generous
3. The Clear and Manifest One
4. The Pure and Perfect
5. The One Most Ready to Appreciate and Reward Abundantly
9. The Appreciative
10. The Forbearing

Down

1. The Generous
3. The One From from All Defects
4. The One Perfect in Glory and Honour
5. The Supremely Glorious
6. The Praiseworthy
11. The True One

Health & Wellness Tips

Health & Wellness Tips

Cultivating a Healthy Mind, Body, and Soul:
Your physical, mental, and spiritual well-being are interconnected, and Ramadhaan is the perfect time to build habits that promote balance and growth in all areas.

Hydration and Nutrition:
Drink water steadily between Iftar and Suhoor (avoid sugary drinks).

Include hydrating foods like cucumbers, melons, and soups.

Plan balanced meals with a mix of protein, vegetables, and whole grains.

Monitor portion sizes to avoid overeating during Iftar.

Avoid heavy, fried foods to prevent sluggishness during fasting.

Health & Wellness Tips

Energy Management:

Avoid unnecessary physical exertion to conserve energy.

Incorporate light exercises like stretching or short walks just before or after Iftar.

Take power naps during the day to recharge energy levels.

Reduce caffeine intake pre-Ramadhaan to prevent withdrawal symptoms.

Sleep Optimization:

Adjust your bedtime to accommodate Suhoor and ensure you get sufficient rest.

Practice good sleep hygiene (e.g., avoid screens before bed, create a relaxing pre-sleep routine).

Encouraging Sustainable Habits

Encouraging Sustainable Habits

Building Long-Term Spiritual Growth:
One of the most significant benefits of Ramadhaan is the opportunity to develop habits that extend far beyond the month itself. Allaah loves consistency in worship and good deeds, as the Prophet Muhammad (ﷺ) said: The most beloved of deeds to Allah are those that are done consistently, even if they are small." (Sahih al-Bukhari 6464, Sahih Muslim 2818)

By focusing on sustainable habits during Ramadhaan, you create a foundation for ongoing personal and spiritual growth. The key is to start small, remain consistent, and prioritize actions that align with your faith.

Steps to Develop Sustainable Habits

1. **Start with Intentions:**
   - Clarify your purpose behind each habit. For example, if you aim to pray Tahajjud regularly, set the intention of seeking closeness to Allaah.
2. **Focus on Consistency:**
   - Incorporate small, manageable actions into your daily routine. For example, commit to reading 1-2 pages of Qur'aan after each prayer instead of overwhelming yourself with an entire Juz.
3. **Track Your Progress:**
   - Use a habit tracker to monitor your consistency in prayer, Qur'aan recitation, and dhikr.
4. **Seek Accountability:**
   - Share your goals with a friend or family member who can support and encourage you.
5. **Reflect and Adjust:**
   - Regularly assess your habits to identify what's working and what needs improvement. Use setbacks as learning opportunities rather than reasons to stop.

Practical Examples of Sustainable Habits

Spiritual Habits:
- Performing the Sunnah prayers consistently.
- Allocating time daily for Qur'aan recitation and tafsir.
- Practicing morning and evening dhikr.

Physical and Mental Habits:
- Drinking sufficient water and maintaining a balanced diet between Iftar and Suhoor.
- Engaging in light physical activity to improve energy levels.
- Taking time to reflect and write down blessings in a gratitude journal.

Social and Charitable Habits:
- Smiling and offering kind words as acts of charity.
- Donating regularly to charitable causes, even if in small amounts.
- Volunteering in the community during and after Ramadhaan.

Habit Trackers

WEEKLY HABIT TRACKER

Habit	Day
	○ ○ ○ ○ ○ ○ ○

Reflecting on Establishing Healthy Habits

Follow these steps to make the most of your habit-building reflections:
1. **Identify Successes:** Write down which habits you were able to maintain consistently and how they impacted your daily life.
2. **Acknowledge Challenges:** Reflect on the habits you struggled with, and explore possible solutions or adjustments.
3. **Set Continuation Goals:** Use your insights to set specific goals for sustaining these habits after Ramadhaan ends.
4. **Be Specific:** Use detailed examples to describe how each habit improved your spiritual, mental, or physical well-being.

Reflective Questions:

- What small changes have had the greatest impact on my spiritual well-being?
- Which habits have been most challenging to maintain, and how can I improve?
- How can I adapt these habits to continue consistently after Ramadhaan?
- What support or resources could help me maintain these habits?

WEEKLY HABIT TRACKER

| Habit | Day |

Reflecting on Establishing Healthy Habits

Follow these steps to make the most of your habit-building reflections:
1. **Identify Successes:** Write down which habits you were able to maintain consistently and how they impacted your daily life.
2. **Acknowledge Challenges:** Reflect on the habits you struggled with, and explore possible solutions or adjustments.
3. **Set Continuation Goals:** Use your insights to set specific goals for sustaining these habits after Ramadhaan ends.
4. **Be Specific:** Use detailed examples to describe how each habit improved your spiritual, mental, or physical well-being.

Reflective Questions:

- What small changes have had the greatest impact on my spiritual well-being?
- Which habits have been most challenging to maintain, and how can I improve?
- How can I adapt these habits to continue consistently after Ramadhaan?
- What support or resources could help me maintain these habits?

WEEKLY HABIT TRACKER

Habit   Day

Reflecting on Establishing Healthy Habits

Follow these steps to make the most of your habit-building reflections:
1. **Identify Successes:** Write down which habits you were able to maintain consistently and how they impacted your daily life.
2. **Acknowledge Challenges:** Reflect on the habits you struggled with, and explore possible solutions or adjustments.
3. **Set Continuation Goals:** Use your insights to set specific goals for sustaining these habits after Ramadhaan ends.
4. **Be Specific:** Use detailed examples to describe how each habit improved your spiritual, mental, or physical well-being.

Reflective Questions:

- What small changes have had the greatest impact on my spiritual well-being?
- Which habits have been most challenging to maintain, and how can I improve?
- How can I adapt these habits to continue consistently after Ramadhaan?
- What support or resources could help me maintain these habits?

WEEKLY HABIT TRACKER

Habit   Day

Reflecting on Establishing Healthy Habits

Follow these steps to make the most of your habit-building reflections:
1. **Identify Successes:** Write down which habits you were able to maintain consistently and how they impacted your daily life.
2. **Acknowledge Challenges:** Reflect on the habits you struggled with, and explore possible solutions or adjustments.
3. **Set Continuation Goals:** Use your insights to set specific goals for sustaining these habits after Ramadhaan ends.
4. **Be Specific:** Use detailed examples to describe how each habit improved your spiritual, mental, or physical well-being.

Reflective Questions:

- What small changes have had the greatest impact on my spiritual well-being?
- Which habits have been most challenging to maintain, and how can I improve?
- How can I adapt these habits to continue consistently after Ramadhaan?
- What support or resources could help me maintain these habits?

_____
_____
_____
_____
_____
_____
_____
_____
_____
_____

WEEKLY HABIT TRACKER

| Habit | Day |

Reflecting on Establishing Healthy Habits

Follow these steps to make the most of your habit-building reflections:
1. **Identify Successes:** Write down which habits you were able to maintain consistently and how they impacted your daily life.
2. **Acknowledge Challenges:** Reflect on the habits you struggled with, and explore possible solutions or adjustments.
3. **Set Continuation Goals:** Use your insights to set specific goals for sustaining these habits after Ramadhaan ends.
4. **Be Specific:** Use detailed examples to describe how each habit improved your spiritual, mental, or physical well-being.

Reflective Questions:

- What small changes have had the greatest impact on my spiritual well-being?
- Which habits have been most challenging to maintain, and how can I improve?
- How can I adapt these habits to continue consistently after Ramadhaan?
- What support or resources could help me maintain these habits?

WEEKLY HABIT TRACKER

Habit	Day
	○ ○ ○ ○ ○ ○ ○
	○ ○ ○ ○ ○ ○ ○
	○ ○ ○ ○ ○ ○ ○
	○ ○ ○ ○ ○ ○ ○
	○ ○ ○ ○ ○ ○ ○
	○ ○ ○ ○ ○ ○ ○
	○ ○ ○ ○ ○ ○ ○
	○ ○ ○ ○ ○ ○ ○
	○ ○ ○ ○ ○ ○ ○
	○ ○ ○ ○ ○ ○ ○
	○ ○ ○ ○ ○ ○ ○
	○ ○ ○ ○ ○ ○ ○
	○ ○ ○ ○ ○ ○ ○
	○ ○ ○ ○ ○ ○ ○
	○ ○ ○ ○ ○ ○ ○
	○ ○ ○ ○ ○ ○ ○
	○ ○ ○ ○ ○ ○ ○
	○ ○ ○ ○ ○ ○ ○
	○ ○ ○ ○ ○ ○ ○
	○ ○ ○ ○ ○ ○ ○
	○ ○ ○ ○ ○ ○ ○
	○ ○ ○ ○ ○ ○ ○
	○ ○ ○ ○ ○ ○ ○
	○ ○ ○ ○ ○ ○ ○
	○ ○ ○ ○ ○ ○ ○
	○ ○ ○ ○ ○ ○ ○

Reflecting on Establishing Healthy Habits

Follow these steps to make the most of your habit-building reflections:
1. **Identify Successes:** Write down which habits you were able to maintain consistently and how they impacted your daily life.
2. **Acknowledge Challenges:** Reflect on the habits you struggled with, and explore possible solutions or adjustments.
3. **Set Continuation Goals:** Use your insights to set specific goals for sustaining these habits after Ramadhaan ends.
4. **Be Specific:** Use detailed examples to describe how each habit improved your spiritual, mental, or physical well-being.

Reflective Questions:

- What small changes have had the greatest impact on my spiritual well-being?
- Which habits have been most challenging to maintain, and how can I improve?
- How can I adapt these habits to continue consistently after Ramadhaan?
- What support or resources could help me maintain these habits?

MONTHLY HABIT TRACKER

Habit | Day

Reflecting on Establishing Healthy Habits

Follow these steps to make the most of your habit-building reflections:
1. **Identify Successes:** Write down which habits you were able to maintain consistently and how they impacted your daily life.
2. **Acknowledge Challenges:** Reflect on the habits you struggled with, and explore possible solutions or adjustments.
3. **Set Continuation Goals:** Use your insights to set specific goals for sustaining these habits after Ramadhaan ends.
4. **Be Specific:** Use detailed examples to describe how each habit improved your spiritual, mental, or physical well-being.

Reflective Questions:

- What positive transformations have I noticed after a month of habit tracking?
- Which habits have become easier to incorporate into my daily routine, and why?
- What lessons did I learn from the challenges of maintaining consistency?
- How has my relationship with Allaah improved through these habits?
- What challenges do I face in maintaining healthy habits, and how can I overcome them?

MONTHLY HABIT TRACKER

Habit | Day

Reflecting on Establishing Healthy Habits

Follow these steps to make the most of your habit-building reflections:
1. **Identify Successes:** Write down which habits you were able to maintain consistently and how they impacted your daily life.
2. **Acknowledge Challenges:** Reflect on the habits you struggled with, and explore possible solutions or adjustments.
3. **Set Continuation Goals:** Use your insights to set specific goals for sustaining these habits after Ramadhaan ends.
4. **Be Specific:** Use detailed examples to describe how each habit improved your spiritual, mental, or physical well-being.

Reflective Questions:

- What positive transformations have I noticed after a month of habit tracking?
- Which habits have become easier to incorporate into my daily routine, and why?
- What lessons did I learn from the challenges of maintaining consistency?
- How has my relationship with Allaah improved through these habits?
- What challenges do I face in maintaining healthy habits, and how can I overcome them?
- What specific habits will I focus on sustaining during Ramadhaan, and how will I do so?

_____
_____
_____
_____
_____
_____
_____
_____

MONTHLY HABIT TRACKER

Habit | Day

Reflecting on Establishing Healthy Habits

Follow these steps to make the most of your habit-building reflections:
1. **Identify Successes:** Write down which habits you were able to maintain consistently and how they impacted your daily life.
2. **Acknowledge Challenges:** Reflect on the habits you struggled with, and explore possible solutions or adjustments.
3. **Set Continuation Goals:** Use your insights to set specific goals for sustaining these habits after Ramadhaan ends.
4. **Be Specific:** Use detailed examples to describe how each habit improved your spiritual, mental, or physical well-being.

Reflective Questions:

- What positive transformations have I noticed after a month of habit tracking?
- Which habits have become easier to incorporate into my daily routine, and why?
- What lessons did I learn from the challenges of maintaining consistency?
- How has my relationship with Allaah improved through these habits?
- What challenges do I face in maintaining healthy habits, and how can I overcome them?
- What specific habits will I focus on sustaining after Ramadhaan, and how will I do so?
- Which new habits have brought me closer to Allaah during Ramadhaan?"

_____
_____
_____
_____
_____
_____
_____
_____

Week 5

Supplication 5: Laylatul Qadr

عَنْ عَائِشَةَ، أَنَّهَا قَالَتْ يَا رَسُولَ اللَّهِ أَرَأَيْتَ إِنْ وَافَقْتُ لَيْلَةَ الْقَدْرِ مَا أَدْعُو قَالَ " تَقُولِينَ اللَّهُمَّ إِنَّكَ عَفُوٌّ تُحِبُّ الْعَفْوَ فَاعْفُ عَنِّي " .

It was narrated from 'Aishah that she said: "O Messenger of Allaah ﷺ, what do you think I should say in my supplication, if I come upon Laylatul-Qadr?" He said: "Say: 'Allahumma innaka 'afuwwun tuhibbul-'afwa, fa'fu 'anni (O Allah, You are Forgiving and love forgiveness, so forgive me)."

Sunan Ibn Majah 3850

Arabic

اللَّهُمَّ إِنَّكَ عَفُوٌّ تُحِبُّ الْعَفْوَ فَاعْفُ عَنِّي

Transliteration

Allahumma innaka 'afuwwun tuhibbul-'afwa, fa'fu 'anni

Word-by-Word

Forgiveness	الْعَفْوَ	Surely You are	إِنَّكَ
So forgive me	فَاعْفُ عَنِّي	Forgiving	عَفُوٌّ
		You love	تُحِبُّ

NOTES:

Week 5: Names of Allaah

القَرِيب
Al-Qareeb
The One Who is Near

المُجِيب
Al-Mujeeb
The Responsive

الْقَاهِر
Al-Qaahir
The Invinvible Subduer

NOTES:

NOTES:

NOTES:

القهّار
Al-Qahhaar
The Overwhelming Subduer

الوارث
Al-Waarith
The Inheritor

المتكبّر
Al-Mutaabbir
The Rightfully Proud

المؤمن
Al-Mu'min
The Giver of Security

NOTES:

NOTES:

NOTES:

الصَّادِق
As-Saadiq
The Truthful

النُّور
An-Noor
The Light

الْمُحْسِن
Al-Muhsin
The One Whose Actions are all Perfect & Good

NOTES:

NOTES:

NOTES:

الدَّيَّان
Ad-Dayyan
The Supreme Judge

الْمُقَدِّم
الْمُؤَخِّر
Al-Muqaddim
Al-Mu'akhkhir
The One Who Gives Precedence & The One Who Puts Back

الطَّيِّب
At-Tayyib
The Pure One

NOTES:

NOTES:

NOTES:

Al Mu'akhkhir	Al Mu'min	Al Mutakabbir	Al Qareeb	Al Muhsin	Ad Dayyaan
Al Qahhaar	Al Waarith	Ash Shaafee	An Noor	Al Mujeeb	Al Qaahir
Al Muqaddim	At Tayyib	As Saadiq			

1. LA EBQREA _ _ _ _ _ _ _

2. LA MEUJEB _ _ _ _ _ _ _

3. LA AHRIAQ _ _ _ _ _ _ _

4. LA HARAQHA _ _ _ _ _ _ _ _

5. LA HAAWTRI _ _ _ _ _ _ _

6. LA BAMIKARTBU _ _ _ _ _ _ _ _ _ _ _ _ _

7. LA NMUMI' _ _ _ _ _ _ _

8. SA IDSAAQ _ _ _ _ _ _

9. NA RONO _ _ _ _ _ _ _

10. LA MHUINS _ _ _ _ _ _ _ _

11. DA AYNYDAA _ _ _ _ _ _ _ _

12. LA MDUMIQAD _ _ _ _ _ _ _ _ _ _ _ _

13. LA KHMIUARK'H _ _ _ _ _ _ _ _

14. TA IAYBTY _ _ _ _ _ _ _

15. HSA SEEFAHA _ _ _ _ _ _ _ _

D	X	K	K	J	L	X	J	H	A	B	B	E	R	I	U
Z	Y	A	N	N	O	O	R	H	I	E	E	I	A	G	O
B	C	T	J	C	E	P	K	Y	E	F	H	R	S	L	C
E	G	X	Q	T	T	C	Y	J	A	K	I	Z	S	Y	A
A	O	J	O	M	S	A	U	A	H	H	N	D	A	E	G
L	K	Q	O	T	M	H	K	A	I	O	W	A	F	J
M	L	L	C	T	L	S	A	A	M	M	G	B	D	H	K
U	Q	T	A	A	H	'	Q	'	L	L	F	J	I	I	R
Q	A	X	O	S	U	L	U	S	E	U	Z	E	Q	K	R
A	H	X	A	M	A	M	H	T	V	M	O	F	B	P	X
D	H	P	L	D	L	U	A	D	D	A	Y	Y	A	A	N
D	A	A	C	A	A	L	M	U	H	S	I	N	Z	R	X
I	A	P	M	G	S	W	L	B	W	G	L	C	W	D	H
M	R	X	M	Z	F	Q	A	L	W	A	A	R	I	T	H
H	R	L	Y	A	L	M	U	T	A	K	A	B	B	I	R
N	A	L	Q	A	R	E	E	B	R	Z	D	Q	A	H	Q

Al Qareeb   Al Mujeeb   Al Qaahir   Al Qahhaar   Al Waarith
Al Mutakabbir   Al Mu'min   As Saadiq   An Noor   Al Muhsin
Ad Dayyaan   Al Muqaddim   Al Mu'akhkhir   At Tayyib   Ash Shaafee

Meal Planners

Meal Planner & Groceries

DATE: /   /

MONDAY

TUESDAY

WEDNESDAY

THURSDAY

FRIDAY

SATURDAY

SUNDAY

GROCERIES:

Meal Planner & Groceries

DATE: / /

MONDAY

TUESDAY

WEDNESDAY

THURSDAY

FRIDAY

SATURDAY

SUNDAY

GROCERIES:

Meal Planner & Groceries

DATE: / /

MONDAY

TUESDAY

WEDNESDAY

THURSDAY

FRIDAY

SATURDAY

SUNDAY

GROCERIES:

- ○
- ○
- ○
- ○
- ○
- ○
- ○
- ○
- ○
- ○
- ○
- ○
- ○
- ○
- ○
- ○
- ○
- ○
- ○
- ○
- ○
- ○
- ○
- ○
- ○
- ○
- ○
- ○

Meal Planner & Groceries

DATE: / /

MONDAY

TUESDAY

WEDNESDAY

THURSDAY

FRIDAY

SATURDAY

SUNDAY

GROCERIES:

-
-
-
-
-
-
-
-
-
-
-
-
-
-
-
-
-
-
-
-
-
-
-
-
-
-
-
-
-
-

Meal Planner & Groceries

DATE: / /

MONDAY

TUESDAY

WEDNESDAY

THURSDAY

FRIDAY

SATURDAY

SUNDAY

GROCERIES:
-
-
-
-
-
-
-
-
-
-
-
-
-
-
-
-
-
-
-
-
-
-
-
-
-
-
-
-
-
-

Meal Planner & Groceries

DATE: / /

MONDAY

TUESDAY

WEDNESDAY

THURSDAY

FRIDAY

SATURDAY

SUNDAY

GROCERIES:

Supplication 6: Du'aa for Repentance

عَنْ أَبِي هُرَيْرَةَ، أَنَّ رَسُولَ اللَّهِ صلى الله عليه وسلم كَانَ يَقُولُ فِي سُجُودِهِ " اللَّهُمَّ اغْفِرْ لِي ذَنْبِي كُلَّهُ دِقَّهُ وَجِلَّهُ وَأَوَّلَهُ وَآخِرَهُ وَعَلاَنِيَتَهُ وَسِرَّهُ " .

Abu Huraira (May Allaah be pleased with him) narrated, The Messenger of Allaah (ﷺ) used to say while prostrating himself: O Lord, forgive me all my sins, small and great, first and last, open and secret.

Arabic

اللَّهُمَّ اغْفِرْ لِي ذَنْبِي كُلَّهُ دِقَّهُ وَجِلَّهُ وَأَوَّلَهُ وَآخِرَهُ وَعَلاَنِيَتَهُ وَسِرَّهُ

Transliteration/Translation

Allāhumma-ghfirlee thanbee kullahu, diqqahu, wa jillahu, wa 'awwalahu, wa ākhirahu, wa alā-niyatahu, wa sirrahu

Word-by-Word

the great of them	وَجِلَّهُ	O Allaah	اللَّهُمَّ
the first of them	وَأَوَّلَهُ	Forgive me	اغْفِرْ لِي
the last of them	وَآخِرَهُ	my sins	ذَنْبِي
the open of them	وَعَلاَنِيَتَهُ	all of them	كُلَّهُ
and the secret of them (the hidden sins)	وَسِرَّهُ	the small of them	دِقَّهُ

NOTES:

Week 6: Names of Allaah

الشَّافِي
Ash-Shaafee

الْجَمِيل
Al-Jameel
The Beautiful

الْقَابِضُ الْبَاسِطُ
Al Qâbid Al Baasit
The Withholder
The Granter of Extensive Provision

NOTES:

NOTES:

NOTES:

الْمَنَّان
Al-Mannaan
The Ever-Bestowing

الْحَيِيّ
Al-Hayyiy
The One Possessing Honorable Shame

السِّتِّير
As-Sitteer
The Concealer of Sins

السَّيِّد
As-Sayyid
The Lord & Master

NOTES:

NOTES:

NOTES:

الرَّفِيق
Ar-Rafeeq
The Gentle

الْوِتْر
Al-Witr
The Singular One

الْمُعْطِي الْجَوَّاد
Al-Mu'tee Al-Jawwad
The Giver The Most Generous

ذُو الْجَلَالُ وَالْإِكْرَام
Dhul Jalaali wal Ikraam

NOTES:

NOTES:

NOTES:

#	Name		Meaning	
1	☐	Al Jameel	And Honour	A
2	☐	Al Qabid	The Beautiful	B
3	☐	Al Baasit	The Withholder	C
4	☐	Al Mannaan	The Giver	D
5	☐	Al Hayyiy	The Ever Bestowing	E
6	☐	As Sitteer	The Gentle	F
7	☐	As Sayyid	Possessing Majesty	G
8	☐	Ar Rafeeq	The One Possessing Honourable	H
9	☐	Al Witr	Shame The Singular One	I
10	☐	Al Mu'tee	The Lord and Master	J
11	☐	Al Jawaad	The Most Generous	K
12	☐	Dhul Jalaali	The Grantor of Extensive Provision	L
13	☐	Wal Ikraam	The Concealer of Sins	M

Across
2. The Beautiful
3. The One Possessing Honourable Shame
6. The Concealer of Sins
8. The Gentle
9. The Singular One
11. The Ever Bestowing
13. And Honour

Dow
12. The Withholder
3. The Grantor of Extensive Provision
7. The Lord and Master
10. The Giver
11. The Most Generous
12. Possessing Majesty

```
D  X  A  E  A  L  J  A  W  A  A  S
H  W  R  A  L  W  I  T  R  E  A  N
U  A  R  P  N  V  T  P  E  D  A  T
L  L  A  Q  X  I  K  T  I  A  I  D
J  I  F  T  S  L  '  Y  N  S  I  A
A  K  E  I  M  U  Y  N  A  B  H  L
L  R  E  G  M  A  A  A  A  U  P  J
A  A  Q  L  S  M  B  Q  L  U  U  A
A  A  A  S  L  L  J  F  F  E  M
L  M  A  A  A  G  P  I  I  G  E
I  A  S  S  I  T  T  E  E  R  G  E
A  L  H  A  Y  Y  I  Y  Z  T  I  L
```

Al Jameel   Al Qabid   Al Baasit   Al Mannaan   Al Hayyiy

As Sitteer   As Sayyid   Ar Rafeeq   Al Witr   Al Mu'tee

Al Jawaas   Dhul Jalaali   Wal Ikraam

| Al Jawaas | Dhul Jalaali wal Ikraam | Al Witr | Al Qabid | Al Mannaan | Ar Rafeeq |
| Al Hayyiy | As Sayyid | Al Mu'tee | Al Jameel | As Sitteer | Al Baasit |

1. LA LEMAJE

2. LA AIDBQ

3. LA ABATIS

4. LA NAAANMN

5. LA YAHIYY

6. SA REISTET

7. SA SYIADY

8. RA RAFQEE

9. LA TRWI

10. LA EUTME

11. LA AAAWJS

12. UDHL IJALALA LWA IRAKMA

Trackers

Weekly Supplication Memorization Tracker

Week	Dua Focus	Progress Notes
1	Upon Seeing the Crescent Moon/New Month	
2	When Breaking the Fast	
3	Qunoot Pt. 1	
4	Qunoot Pt. 2	
5	Laylatul Qadr	
6	Repentance	

Names of Allaah Memorization Tracker

Name of Allaah   **Progress Notes/Reflection**

Ar-Rabb - The Lord

Ar-Rahmaan - The Most Merciful

Ar-Raheem - The Bestower of Mercy

Al-Hayy - The Ever-Living

Al-Qayyoom - The Self-Subsiting Sustainer

Names of Allaah Memorization Tracker

Name of Allaah   **Progress Notes/Reflection**

Al-Khaaliq- The Creator

Al-Khallaaq - The Ever-Creating

Al-Baari - The Originator

Al-Musawwir - The Fashioner

Al-Malik - The King

Names of Allaah Memorization Tracker

Name of Allaah   **Progress Notes/Reflection**

Al-Maleek - The Supreme Sovereign

Ar-Razzaaq - The Great Provider

Ar-Raaziq - The Best of Sustainers

Al-Ahad - The Unique

Al-Waahid - The One

Names of Allaah Memorization Tracker

Name of Allaah	Progress Notes/Reflection
As-Samad - The Self-Sufficient Master	
Al-Haadee - The Guide	
Al-Wahhaab - The Bestower	
Al-Fattaah - The Just Judge	
As-Samee' - The All-Hearing	

Names of Allaah Memorization Tracker

Name of Allaah **Progress Notes/Reflection**

Al-Baseer - The All-Seeing

Al-'Aleem - The All-Knowing

Al-Lateef - The Subtle & Kind

Al-Khabeer - The Fully Aware

Al-'Afw - The Pardoner

Names of Allaah Memorization Tracker

Name of Allaah   **Progress Notes/Reflection**

Al-Ghafoor - The Ever-Forgiving

Al-'Alee - The Exalted

Al-'Alaa - The Most High

Al-Muta'aal - The Supreme and Exalted One

Al-Kabeer - The Most Great

Names of Allaah Memorization Tracker

Name of Allaah	Progress Notes/Reflection
Al-'Adheem - The Magnificent	
Al-Qawee - The One Perfect in Strength	
Al-Mateen - The Strong	
Ash-Shaheed - The Witness	
Ar-Raqeeb - The Ever-Watchful Guardian	

Names of Allaah Memorization Tracker

Name of Allaah	Progress Notes/Reflection
Al-Muhaymin - The Ever-Watchful Witness	
Al-Muheet - The All-Encompassing	
Al-Muqeet - The All-Powerful Maintainer and Guardian	
Al-Waasi' - The Vast One	
Al-Hafeedth - The Guardian and Preserver	

Names of Allaah Memorization Tracker

Name of Allaah **Progress Notes/Reflection**

Al-Haafidh - The Protector

Al-Walee - The Protector

Al-Mawlaa - The Protector and Supporter

Al-Awwal, Al-Aakhir - The First, The Last

Adh-Dhaahir Al-Baatin - The Uppermost, The Closet One

Names of Allaah Memorization Tracker

Name of Allaah	Progress Notes/Reflection
Al-Hakeem - The All-Wise	
Al-Ghanee - The Rich Free of All Need	
Al-Kareem - The Generous	
Al-Akram - The Most Generous	
As-Salaam - The One Free from all Defects	

Names of Allaah Memorization Tracker

Name of Allaah   **Progress Notes/Reflection**

Al-Quddoos - The Pure and Perfect

As-Subbooh - The Supremely Glorious

Al-Hameed - The Praiseworthy

Al-Majeed - The One Perfect in Glory and Honour

Ash-Shakoor - The One Most Ready to Appreciate & Reward Abundantly

Names of Allaah Memorization Tracker

Name of Allaah **Progress Notes/Reflection**

Ash-Shaakir - The Appreciative

Al-Haleem - The Forbearing

Al-Haqq - The True One

Al-Mubeen - The Clear and Manifest One

Al-Qadeer - The All-Powerful

Names of Allaah Memorization Tracker

Name of Allaah   **Progress Notes/Reflection**

Al-Qaadir - The Fully Able

Al-Muqtadir - The All-Capable

Al-Wadood - The Loving & The Beloved

Al-Barr - The Most Benign & Kind

Ar-Ra'oof - The Compassionate & Kind

Names of Allaah Memorization Tracker

Name of Allaah **Progress Notes/Reflection**

Al-Haseeb - The Reckoner Who Suffices

Al-Kaafee - The Sufficient

Al-Kafeel - The Witness

Al-Wakeel - The Guardian/Disposer of Affairs

Al-Ghaalib - The Predominant

Names of Allaah Memorization Tracker

Name of Allaah   **Progress Notes/Reflection**

An-Naseer - The Helper

Al-Azeez - The Almighty

Al-Jabbaar - The Exalted and Almighty Compeller

Al-Qareeb - The One Who is Near

Al-Mujeeb - The Responsive

Names of Allaah Memorization Tracker

Name of Allaah	Progress Notes/Reflection
Al-Qaahir - The Invincible Subduer	
Al-Qahhar - The Overwhelming Subduer	
Al-Waarith - The Inheritor	
Al-Mutakabbir - The Rightfully Proud	
Al-Mu'min - The Giver of Security	

Names of Allaah Memorization Tracker

Name of Allaah   **Progress Notes/Reflection**

As-Saadiq - The Truthful

An-Noor - The Light

Al-Muhsin - The One Whose Actions are all Perfect & Good

Ad-Dayyaan - The Supreme Judge

Al-Muqaddim Al-Mu'akhkhir - The One Who Gives Precendence & The One Who Puts Back

Names of Allaah Memorization Tracker

Name of Allaah	Progress Notes/Reflection
At-Tayyib - The Pure One	
Ash-Shaafee - The One Who Cures	
Al-Jameel - The Beautiful	
Al-Qabid Al Baasit - The Withholder, The Granter of Extensive Provision	
Al-Mannaan - The Ever-Bestowing	

Names of Allaah Memorization Tracker

Name of Allaah   **Progress Notes/Reflection**

Al-Hayyiy - The One Possessing Honorable Shame

As-Sitteer - The Concealer of Sins

As-Sayyid - The Lord & Master

Ar-Rafeeq - the Gentle

Al-Witr - The Singular One

Names of Allaah Memorization Tracker

Name of Allaah   **Progress Notes/Reflection**

Al-Mu'tee – The Giver

Al-Jawwad – The Most Generous

Dhul Jalaali wal-Ikraam – Possessing Majesty & Honor

عَنْ أَبِي هُرَيْرَةَ، أَنَّ رَسُولَ اللَّهِ صلى الله عليه وسلم قَالَ "إِنَّ لِلَّهِ تِسْعَةً وَتِسْعِينَ اسْمًا مِائَةً إِلاَّ وَاحِدًا، مَنْ أَحْصَاهَا دَخَلَ الْجَنَّةَ". {أَحْصَيْنَاهُ} حَفِظْنَاهُ.

Narrated Abu Huraira (May Allaah be pleased with him): Allaah's Messenger (ﷺ) said, "Allaah has ninety-nine Names, one-hundred less one; and he who memorized them all by heart will enter Paradise." To count something means to know it by heart.
Bukhari 7392

The Qur'aan is not just a book to be read; it is a divine guide sent by Allaah the Sublime, to illuminate our hearts, shape our character, and inspire our actions. Allaah describes the Qur'aan as:

كِتَٰبٌ أَنزَلْنَٰهُ إِلَيْكَ مُبَٰرَكٌ لِّيَدَّبَّرُوٓا۟ ءَايَٰتِهِۦ وَلِيَتَذَكَّرَ أُو۟لُوا۟ ٱلْأَلْبَٰبِ

[This is] a blessed Book which We have revealed to you, [O Muḥammad], that they might reflect upon its verses and that those of understanding would be reminded. {Sad:29}

This verse highlights the importance of reflecting (taddabur) on the Qur'an. Its message is not merely to be recited but to be understood and implemented in our daily lives.

The Qur'aan is described as "light" and "healing". It illuminates the path of righteousness and heals the wounds of the heart. Each verse is a mirror, reflecting both the beauty of Allaah's creation and the areas where we can improve ourselves.

Allaah says in Suratul Isra: 9

"Verily, this Qur'aan guides to that which is most just and right and gives glad tidings to the believers (in the Oneness of Allaah and His Messenger, Muhammad ﷺ), who work deeds of righteousness, that they shall have a great reward (Paradise)."

Let the Qur'aan be your companion, not only in Ramadhaan but throughout your life. Strive to recite it, reflect upon it, and act upon its teachings. In doing so, you will find peace, guidance, and closeness to Allaah.

May Allaah make us among those who recite, reflect and live by the Qur'aan. Aameen.

What is Taddabur?

Taddabur is the act of deep reflection and pondering over the meanings, wisdom, and lessons in the Qur'aan. It involves connecting with the words of Allaah on a deeper level, allowing the heart to absorb its guidance. Through taddabur, the Qur'aan transforms from a recitation into a living guide that impacts every aspect of our lives.

Benefits of Reflecting on the Qur'aan:

- **Strengthens Faith (Imaan):** Reflecting on the verses of the Qur'aan strengthens our belief in Allaah's wisdom, power, and mercy. It deepens our understanding of His creation and the purpose of our existence.
- **Guides Decision-Making:** The Qur'aan offers timeless wisdom that helps us navigate life's challenges with clarity and confidence. Reflection allows us to align our decisions with Allaah's commands.
- **Purifies the Heart:** Pondering over the Qur'aan helps us recognize our shortcomings and inspires us to improve. It purifies the heart of arrogance, heedlessness, and doubt.
- **Inspires Gratitude and Patience:** The Qur'aan reminds us of Allaah's countless blessings and the reward for those who remain patient through trials. Reflection nurtures gratitude and perseverance in worship.
- **Fosters Spiritual Growth:** By contemplating the Qur'aan, we gain insights that deepen our connection to Allaah and foster a sense of accountability in our actions.

How to Reflect on the Qur'aan

Read with Intention: Begin with a sincere intention to seek guidance and understanding from Allaah. Make dua for Allaah to open your heart to His words.

Focus on Quality, Not Quantity: It is better to read a few verses and reflect deeply than to rush through pages without understanding. Pause and ponder over the meanings of the verses.

Use Tafsir (Explanation): Refer to authentic tafsir to understand the historical context, linguistic nuances, and deeper meanings of the verses.

Ask Questions: As you read, ask yourself: What is Allaah teaching me in this verse? How can I apply this lesson in my life? What changes should I make to align with this guidance?

Write Reflections: Keep a journal to record insights, lessons, and personal reflections from your Qur'aanic reading. This helps solidify your understanding and allows you to revisit your thoughts later.

Take Action: Reflection without implementation is incomplete. Let the Qur'aan inspire you to make positive changes in your worship, relationships, and character.

The Virtues of Qur'aan Reading

Every Letter Brings Reward:
The Prophet Muhammad (ﷺ) said: "Whoever recites a letter from the Book of Allaah, he will be credited with a good deed, and a good deed gets a tenfold reward. I do not say that Alif-Lam-Meem is one letter, but Alif is a letter, Lam is a letter, and Meem is a letter." (Sunan At-Tirmidhi 2910)

A Source of Light:
The Qur'an is described as a light guiding believers through the darkness of life. Allaah says: "So believe in Allaah and His Messenger and the Qur'aan which We have sent down. And Allaah is All-Aware of what you do." (Surah At-Taghabun, 64:8)

Elevates Status in the Hereafter:
The Prophet (ﷺ) said: "The one who recites the Qur'an and acts upon it will be told on the Day of Resurrection, 'Recite and ascend, and recite as you used to recite in the world, for your position will be at the last verse you recite.'" (Sunan Abi Dawood 1464)

Brings Peace and Tranquility:
The Qur'aan soothes the hearts of those who recite and reflect on it. Allaah says: "Indeed, by the remembrance of Allaah do hearts find rest." (Surah Ar-Ra'd, 13:28)

The Virtues of Qur'aan Reading

The Significance of Qur'aan Reading in Ramadhaan: Ramadhaan is the month in which the Qur'aan was revealed as a guidance for mankind. Allaah says:

شَهْرُ رَمَضَانَ ٱلَّذِىٓ أُنزِلَ فِيهِ ٱلْقُرْءَانُ هُدًى لِّلنَّاسِ وَبَيِّنَـٰتٍ مِّنَ ٱلْهُدَىٰ وَٱلْفُرْقَانِ

The month of Ramadhaan [is that] in which was revealed the Qur'aan, a guidance for the people, and clear proofs of guidance and criterion." (Surah Al-Baqarah, 2:185)

The Prophet Muhammad (ﷺ) emphasized the virtues of reciting and reflecting on the Qur'aan: "Recite the Qur'aan, for it will come as an intercessor for its reciters on the Day of Resurrection." (Sahih Muslim 804)

By incorporating Qur'aan reading into your daily routine, you can deepen your connection with Allaah and reap the blessings of this holy month.

How the Salaf Completed the Qur'aan

The righteous predecessors (Salaf) set examples of dedication to the Qur'aan during Ramadhaan:
Imam Shafi'i: He completed the Qur'an 60 times during Ramadhaan.

Uthman ibn Affan (May Allaah be pleased with him): It is narrated that he would complete the entire Qur'aan in one night of prayer.

Other Companions and Scholars: Many of them would dedicate their days and nights to recitation, tafsir, and reflection, minimizing worldly distractions.

While these examples are inspiring, focus on your personal capacity and consistency, aiming to complete the Qur'aan or recite as much as possible while maintaining khushu' (devotion).

The Gift of the Qur'an

The Qur'aan is not merely a book; it is a divine letter of guidance, mercy, and light from Allaah to humanity. Completing its recitation, especially during Ramadhaan, is a spiritual journey that transforms the heart, mind, and soul. Whether you aim to complete it in 10, 15, or 30 days, each step in this journey brings you closer to Allaah and deepens your connection to His words.

The Rewards of Consistency

No matter the timeline you choose, consistency is key. Allaah rewards effort, no matter how small or large. As previously mentioned, The Prophet (ﷺ) said: "The most beloved of deeds to Allaah are those that are done consistently, even if they are small." (Sahih al-Bukhari 6464, Sahih Muslim 2818)

- Whether you finish in 10 days or 30 days, the journey through the Qur'aan transforms your Ramadhaan into a month of profound growth and closeness to Allaah.
- Let your intention be sincere: to seek Allaah's pleasure and to live by His words. The time you dedicate now will echo in your deeds, shaping your heart and actions for the months to come.

The next few pages will consist of 10, 15, & 30 Day trackers that you can use to track your reading progress.

Tips for Effective Qur'aan Reading

1. **Set a Schedule:** Divide your daily reading into manageable portions (e.g., 5 pages after each prayer).
2. **Reflect on the Meanings:** Use tafsir or translations to understand the verses.
3. **Prioritize Quality over Quantity:** Strive for heartfelt recitation, even if it means reading less.
4. **Make Du'a Before Reading:** Ask Allaah to open your heart to His words and grant you understanding.

30-Day Khatm (Completion) Qur'aan Tracker

Completing the Qur'aan in 30 Days

A 30-day plan, reciting one Juz daily, reflects the prophetic tradition of consistent, deliberate worship. It aligns beautifully with the daily prayers, creating a natural rhythm for your Qur'aanic connection.

- Dividing each Juz into five parts to recite after the five daily prayers transforms your salah into moments of deeper reflection and gratitude.
- The Prophet Muhammad (ﷺ) said: "Recite the Qur'aan, for it will come as an intercessor for its companions on the Day of Resurrection." (Sahih Muslim 804) Each day, you remind yourself that every word you recite is a step closer to this intercession.

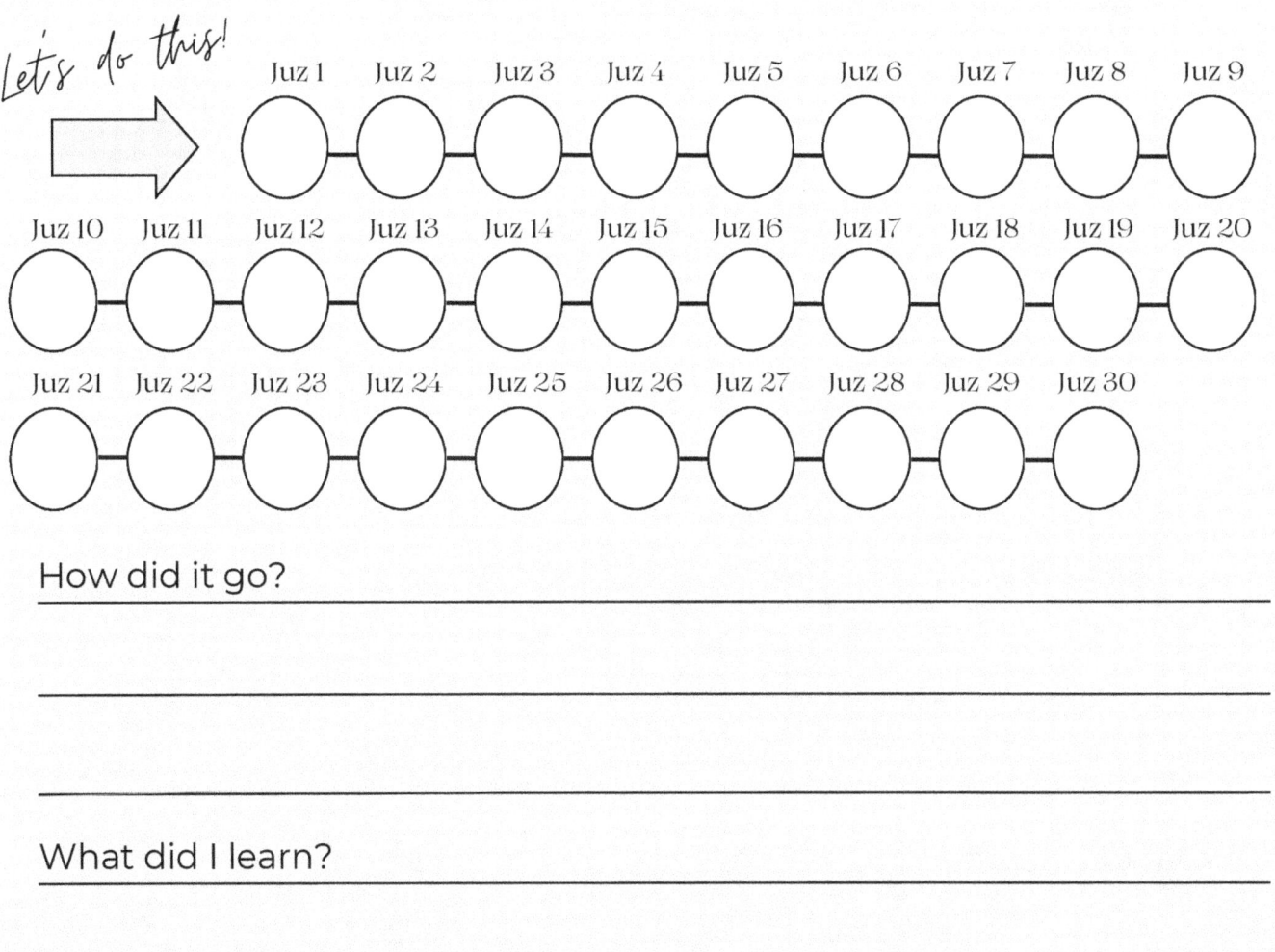

How did it go?

What did I learn?

30-Day Khatm (Completion) Qur'aan Tracker

Completing the Qur'aan in 30 Days

A 30-day plan, reciting one Juz daily, reflects the prophetic tradition of consistent, deliberate worship. It aligns beautifully with the daily prayers, creating a natural rhythm for your Qur'aanic connection.

- Dividing each Juz into five parts to recite after the five daily prayers transforms your salah into moments of deeper reflection and gratitude.
- The Prophet Muhammad (ﷺ) said: "Recite the Qur'aan, for it will come as an intercessor for its companions on the Day of Resurrection." (Sahih Muslim 804) Each day, you remind yourself that every word you recite is a step closer to this intercession.

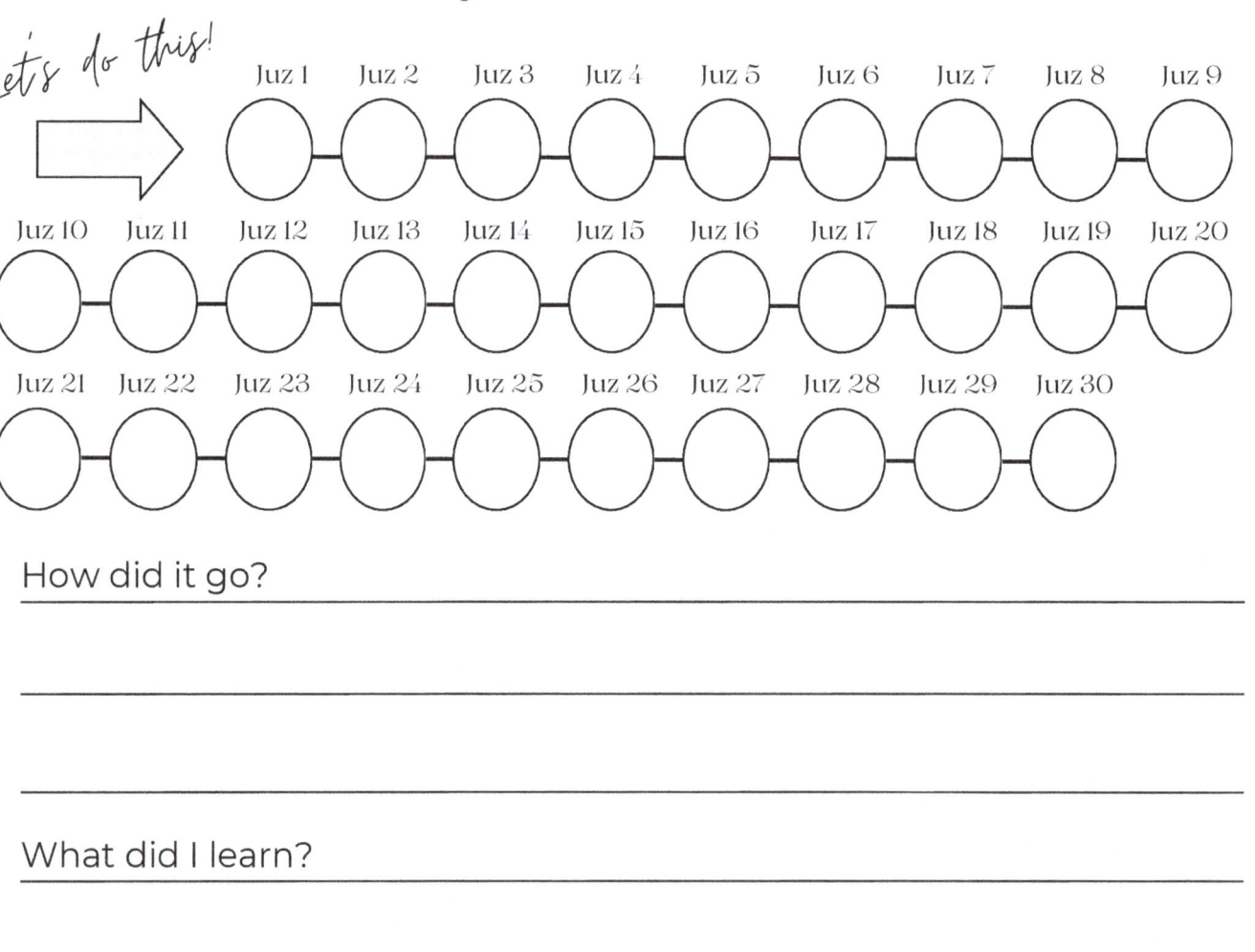

How did it go?
_____
_____
_____

What did I learn?
_____
_____
_____

30-Day Khatm (Completion) Qur'aan Tracker

Completing the Qur'aan in 30 Days

A 30-day plan, reciting one Juz daily, reflects the prophetic tradition of consistent, deliberate worship. It aligns beautifully with the daily prayers, creating a natural rhythm for your Qur'aanic connection.

- Dividing each Juz into five parts to recite after the five daily prayers transforms your salah into moments of deeper reflection and gratitude.
- The Prophet Muhammad (ﷺ) said: "Recite the Qur'aan, for it will come as an intercessor for its companions on the Day of Resurrection." (Sahih Muslim 804) Each day, you remind yourself that every word you recite is a step closer to this intercession.

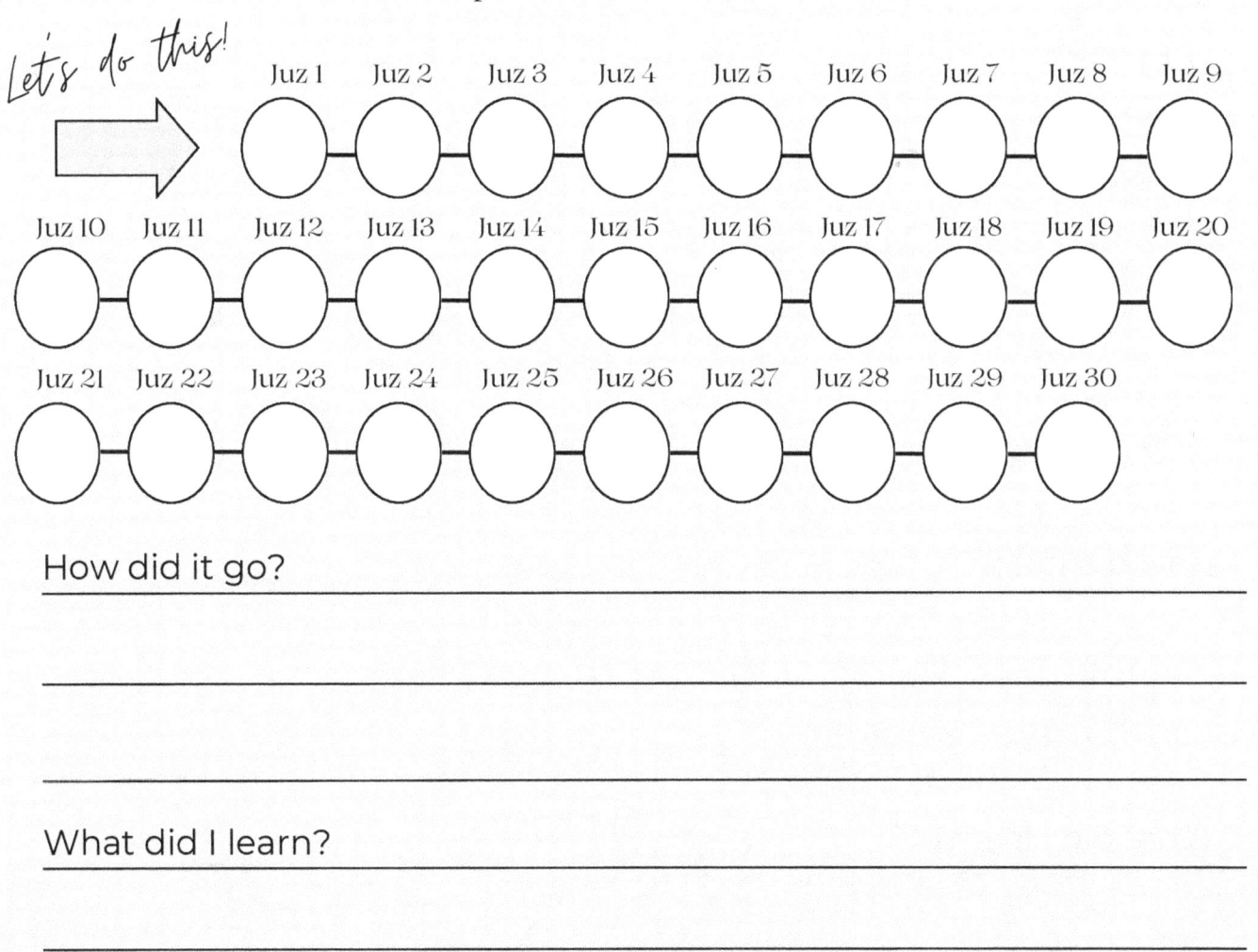

How did it go?
_____
_____
_____

What did I learn?
_____
_____
_____

30-Day Khatm (Completion) Qur'aan Tracker

Completing the Qur'aan in 30 Days

A 30-day plan, reciting one Juz daily, reflects the prophetic tradition of consistent, deliberate worship. It aligns beautifully with the daily prayers, creating a natural rhythm for your Qur'aanic connection.

- Dividing each Juz into five parts to recite after the five daily prayers transforms your salah into moments of deeper reflection and gratitude.
- The Prophet Muhammad (ﷺ) said: "Recite the Qur'aan, for it will come as an intercessor for its companions on the Day of Resurrection." (Sahih Muslim 804) Each day, you remind yourself that every word you recite is a step closer to this intercession.

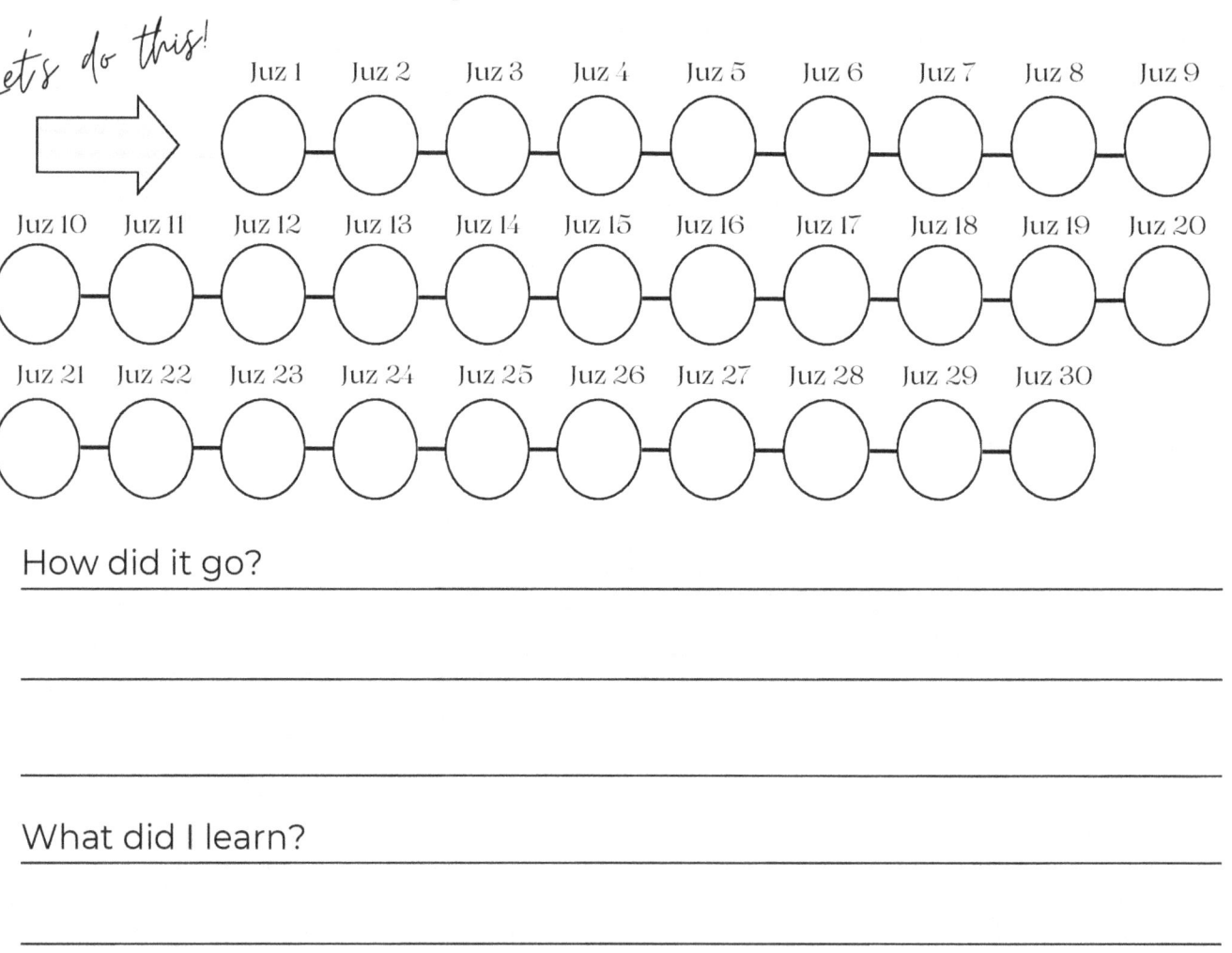

How did it go?
_____
_____
_____

What did I learn?
_____
_____
_____

30-Day Khatm (Completion) Qur'aan Tracker

Completing the Qur'aan in 30 Days

A 30-day plan, reciting one Juz daily, reflects the prophetic tradition of consistent, deliberate worship. It aligns beautifully with the daily prayers, creating a natural rhythm for your Qur'aanic connection.

- Dividing each Juz into five parts to recite after the five daily prayers transforms your salah into moments of deeper reflection and gratitude.
- The Prophet Muhammad (ﷺ) said: "Recite the Qur'aan, for it will come as an intercessor for its companions on the Day of Resurrection." (Sahih Muslim 804) Each day, you remind yourself that every word you recite is a step closer to this intercession.

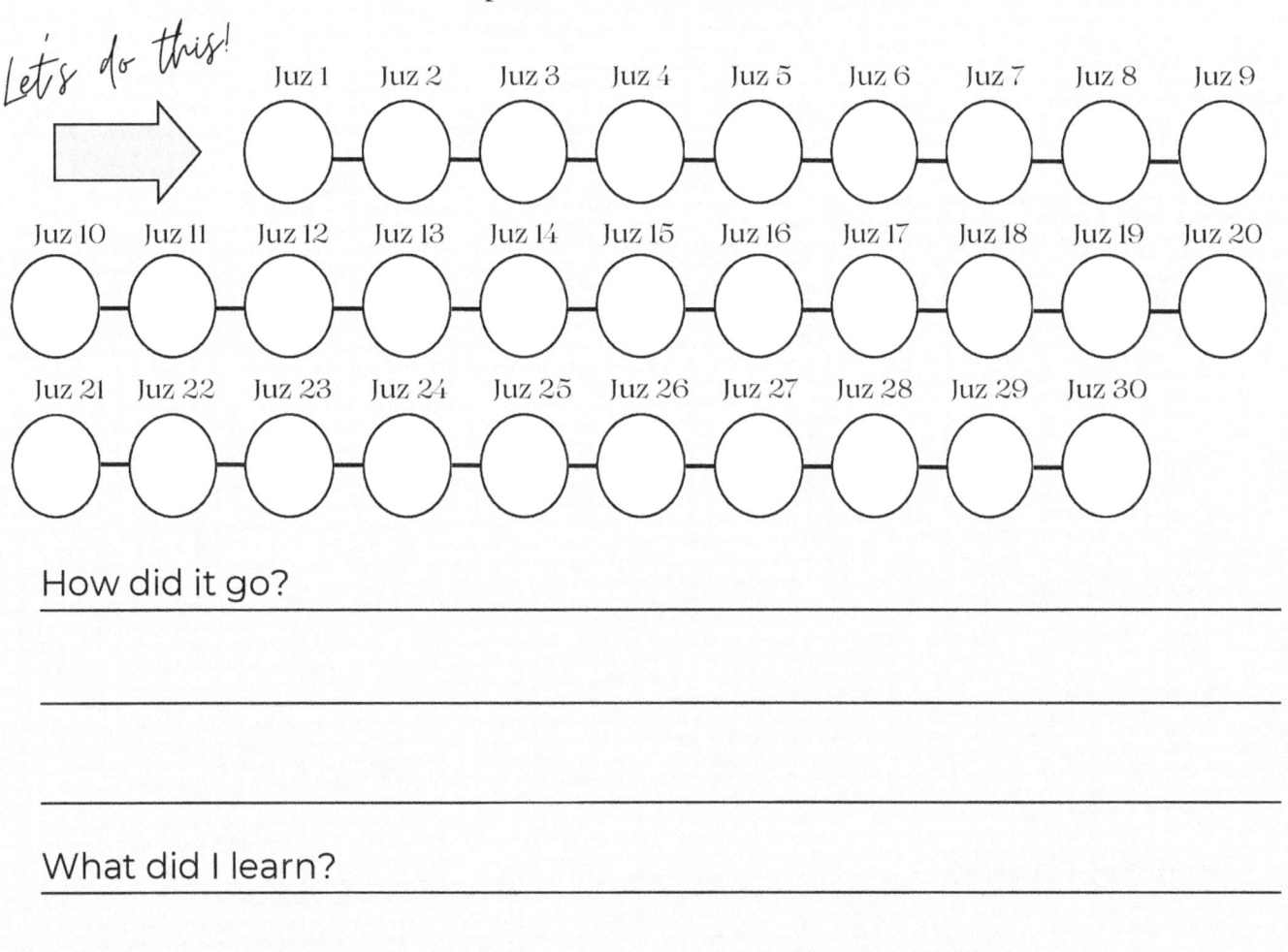

How did it go?
_____

_____

_____

What did I learn?
_____

_____

_____

30-Day Khatm (Completion) Qur'aan Tracker

Completing the Qur'aan in 30 Days

A 30-day plan, reciting one Juz daily, reflects the prophetic tradition of consistent, deliberate worship. It aligns beautifully with the daily prayers, creating a natural rhythm for your Qur'aanic connection.

- Dividing each Juz into five parts to recite after the five daily prayers transforms your salah into moments of deeper reflection and gratitude.
- The Prophet Muhammad (ﷺ) said: "Recite the Qur'aan, for it will come as an intercessor for its companions on the Day of Resurrection." (Sahih Muslim 804) Each day, you remind yourself that every word you recite is a step closer to this intercession.

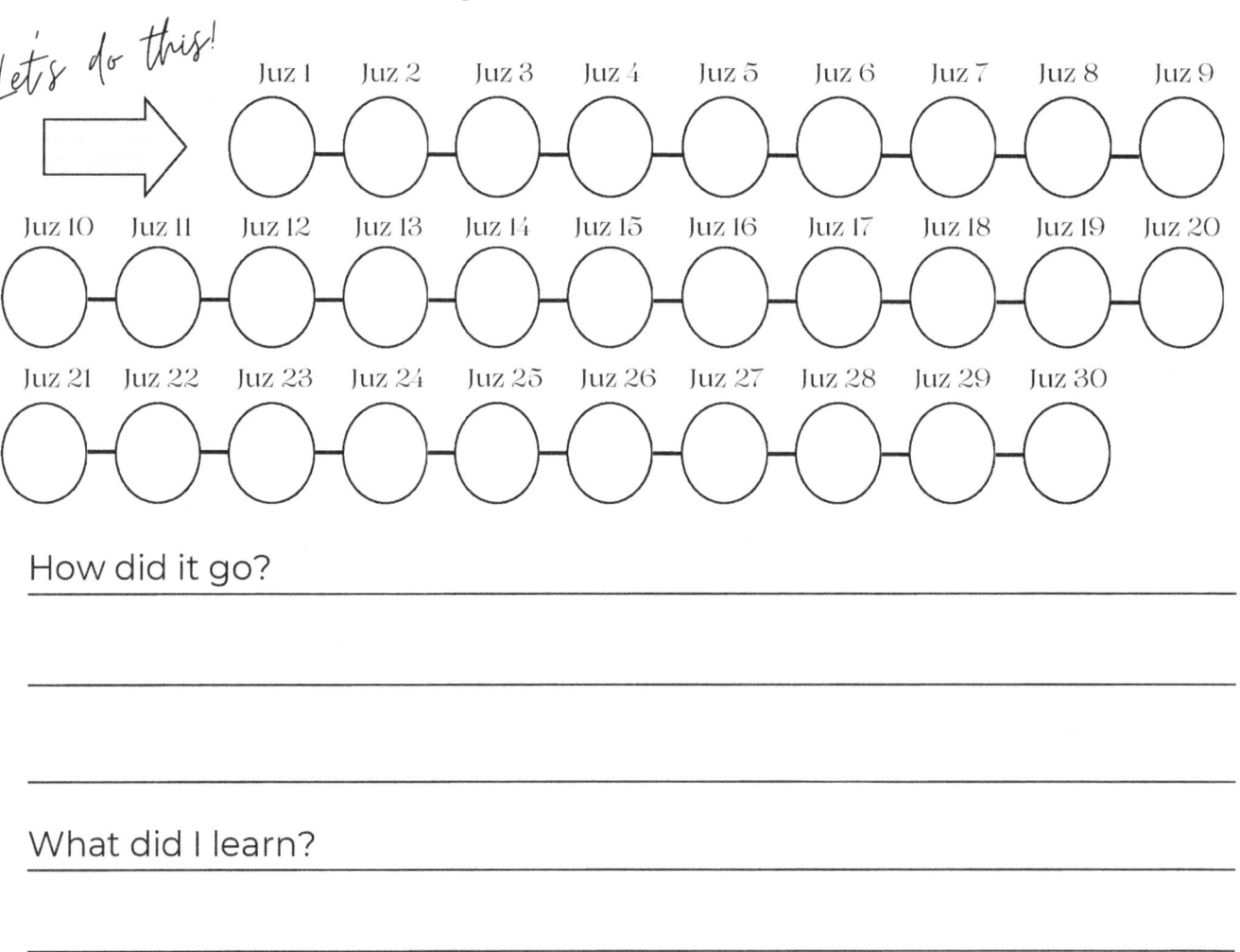

How did it go? _____

_____

_____

What did I learn? _____

_____

_____

15-Day Khatm (Completion) Qur'aan Tracker

Completing the Qur'an in 15 Days

A 15-day plan balances spiritual intensity and manageable pacing, allowing you to reflect deeply on the verses while maintaining steady progress.

- Each day, you complete two Juz, a rhythm that fosters both consistency and spiritual reflection. As you recite, you ponder over the meanings of Allaah's words, letting their wisdom sink into your heart.
- Allaah says: "And We have certainly made the Qur'aan easy for remembrance, so is there any who will remember?" (Surah Al-Qamar, 54:17). This pace reminds you that with sincerity and determination, Allaah facilitates your journey to His book

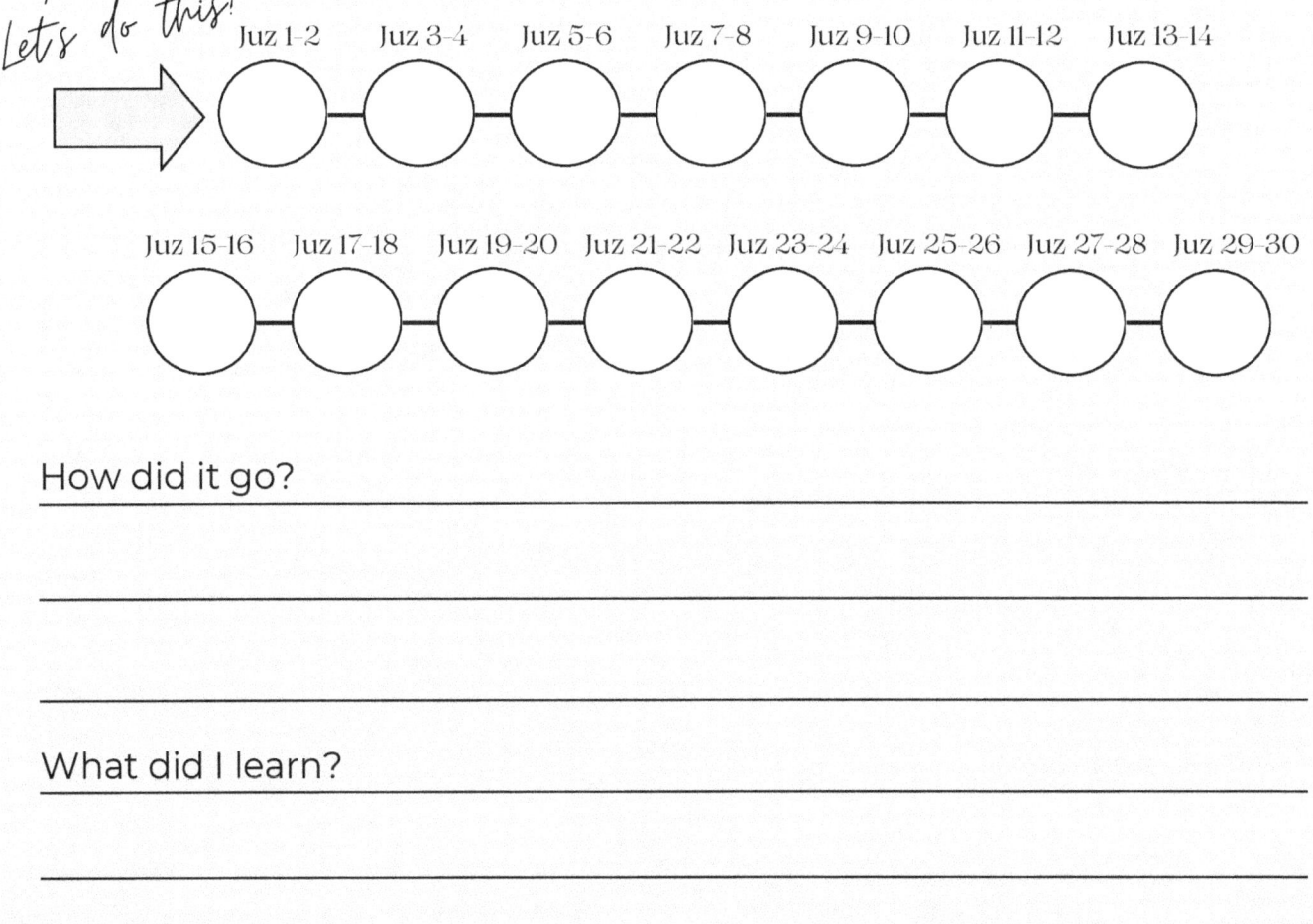

How did it go? _____
_____
_____

What did I learn? _____
_____
_____

15-Day Khatm (Completion) Qur'aan Tracker

Completing the Qur'an in 15 Days

A 15-day plan balances spiritual intensity and manageable pacing, allowing you to reflect deeply on the verses while maintaining steady progress.

- Each day, you complete two Juz, a rhythm that fosters both consistency and spiritual reflection. As you recite, you ponder over the meanings of Allaah's words, letting their wisdom sink into your heart.
- Allaah says: "And We have certainly made the Qur'aan easy for remembrance, so is there any who will remember?" (Surah Al-Qamar, 54:17). This pace reminds you that with sincerity and determination, Allaah facilitates your journey to His book

Let's do this! → Juz 1-2 ○ — Juz 3-4 ○ — Juz 5-6 ○ — Juz 7-8 ○ — Juz 9-10 ○ — Juz 11-12 ○ — Juz 13-14 ○

Juz 15-16 ○ — Juz 17-18 ○ — Juz 19-20 ○ — Juz 21-22 ○ — Juz 23-24 ○ — Juz 25-26 ○ — Juz 27-28 ○ — Juz 29-30 ○

How did it go?
_____
_____
_____

What did I learn?
_____
_____
_____

15-Day Khatm (Completion) Qur'aan Tracker

Completing the Qur'an in 15 Days

A 15-day plan balances spiritual intensity and manageable pacing, allowing you to reflect deeply on the verses while maintaining steady progress.

- Each day, you complete two Juz, a rhythm that fosters both consistency and spiritual reflection. As you recite, you ponder over the meanings of Allaah's words, letting their wisdom sink into your heart.
- Allaah says: "And We have certainly made the Qur'aan easy for remembrance, so is there any who will remember?" (Surah Al-Qamar, 54:17). This pace reminds you that with sincerity and determination, Allaah facilitates your journey to His book

Let's do this!

Juz 1-2 ○ — Juz 3-4 ○ — Juz 5-6 ○ — Juz 7-8 ○ — Juz 9-10 ○ — Juz 11-12 ○ — Juz 13-14 ○

Juz 15-16 ○ — Juz 17-18 ○ — Juz 19-20 ○ — Juz 21-22 ○ — Juz 23-24 ○ — Juz 25-26 ○ — Juz 27-28 ○ — Juz 29-30 ○

How did it go? _____

_____

_____

What did I learn? _____

_____

_____

15-Day Khatm (Completion) Qur'aan Tracker

Completing the Qur'an in 15 Days

A 15-day plan balances spiritual intensity and manageable pacing, allowing you to reflect deeply on the verses while maintaining steady progress.

- Each day, you complete two Juz, a rhythm that fosters both consistency and spiritual reflection. As you recite, you ponder over the meanings of Allaah's words, letting their wisdom sink into your heart.
- Allaah says: "And We have certainly made the Qur'aan easy for remembrance, so is there any who will remember?" (Surah Al-Qamar, 54:17). This pace reminds you that with sincerity and determination, Allaah facilitates your journey to His book

Let's do this! → Juz 1-2 — Juz 3-4 — Juz 5-6 — Juz 7-8 — Juz 9-10 — Juz 11-12 — Juz 13-14

Juz 15-16 — Juz 17-18 — Juz 19-20 — Juz 21-22 — Juz 23-24 — Juz 25-26 — Juz 27-28 — Juz 29-30

How did it go?
_____
_____
_____

What did I learn?
_____
_____
_____

15-Day Khatm (Completion) Qur'aan Tracker

Completing the Qur'an in 15 Days

A 15-day plan balances spiritual intensity and manageable pacing, allowing you to reflect deeply on the verses while maintaining steady progress.

- Each day, you complete two Juz, a rhythm that fosters both consistency and spiritual reflection. As you recite, you ponder over the meanings of Allaah's words, letting their wisdom sink into your heart.
- Allaah says: "And We have certainly made the Qur'aan easy for remembrance, so is there any who will remember?" (Surah Al-Qamar, 54:17). This pace reminds you that with sincerity and determination, Allaah facilitates your journey to His book

Let's do this!

Juz 1-2 Juz 3-4 Juz 5-6 Juz 7-8 Juz 9-10 Juz 11-12 Juz 13-14

Juz 15-16 Juz 17-18 Juz 19-20 Juz 21-22 Juz 23-24 Juz 25-26 Juz 27-28 Juz 29-30

How did it go? _____
_____
_____

What did I learn? _____
_____
_____

15-Day Khatm (Completion) Qur'aan Tracker

Completing the Qur'an in 15 Days
A 15-day plan balances spiritual intensity and manageable pacing, allowing you to reflect deeply on the verses while maintaining steady progress.

- Each day, you complete two Juz, a rhythm that fosters both consistency and spiritual reflection. As you recite, you ponder over the meanings of Allaah's words, letting their wisdom sink into your heart.
- Allaah says: "And We have certainly made the Qur'aan easy for remembrance, so is there any who will remember?" (Surah Al-Qamar, 54:17). This pace reminds you that with sincerity and determination, Allaah facilitates your journey to His book

Let's do this! → Juz 1-2 ○—Juz 3-4 ○—Juz 5-6 ○—Juz 7-8 ○—Juz 9-10 ○—Juz 11-12 ○—Juz 13-14 ○

Juz 15-16 ○—Juz 17-18 ○—Juz 19-20 ○—Juz 21-22 ○—Juz 23-24 ○—Juz 25-26 ○—Juz 27-28 ○—Juz 29-30 ○

How did it go?
_____
_____
_____

What did I learn?
_____
_____
_____

10-Day Khatm (Completion) Qur'aan Tracker

Completing the Qur'aan in 10 Days:

A 10-day Qur'aan completion requires dedication and focus, making it an intense and spiritually uplifting endeavor. Each day involves reciting three Juz, immersing you deeply into the flow of the Qur'aan's powerful messages.

- "This is a month of striving," you remind yourself as you prioritize time for recitation above all else. Imagine completing the Qur'aan not once, but three times during Ramadhaan, multiplying the barakah and rewards.
- The Prophet Muhammad (peace be upon him) said: "The best of you are those who learn the Qur'aan and teach it." (Sahih al-Bukhari 5027) In this pursuit, you not only elevate your own faith but inspire others to embark on a similar journey.

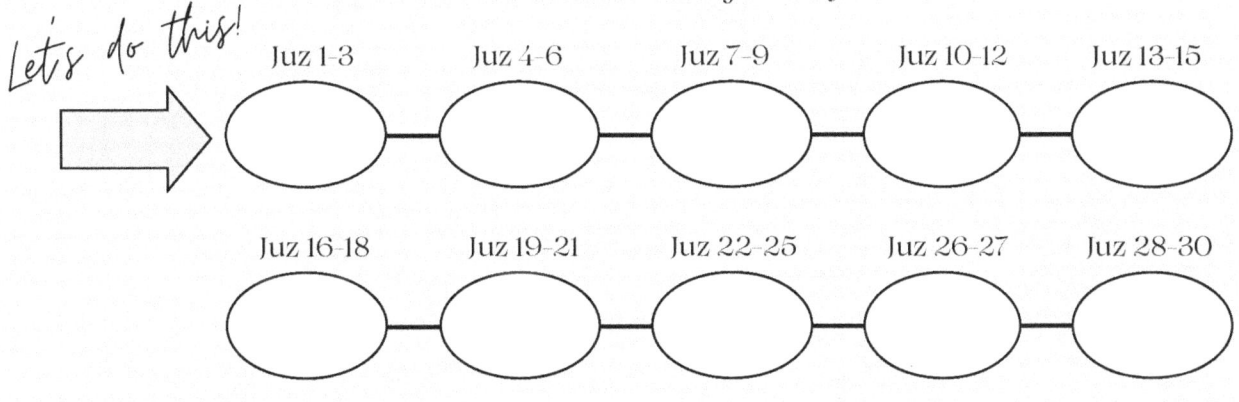

How did it go?
_____
_____
_____

What did I learn?
_____
_____
_____

10-Day Khatm (Completion) Qur'aan Tracker

Completing the Qur'aan in 10 Days:
A 10-day Qur'aan completion requires dedication and focus, making it an intense and spiritually uplifting endeavor. Each day involves reciting three Juz, immersing you deeply into the flow of the Qur'aan's powerful messages.

- "This is a month of striving," you remind yourself as you prioritize time for recitation above all else. Imagine completing the Qur'aan not once, but three times during Ramadhaan, multiplying the barakah and rewards.
- The Prophet Muhammad (peace be upon him) said: "The best of you are those who learn the Qur'aan and teach it." (Sahih al-Bukhari 5027) In this pursuit, you not only elevate your own faith but inspire others to embark on a similar journey.

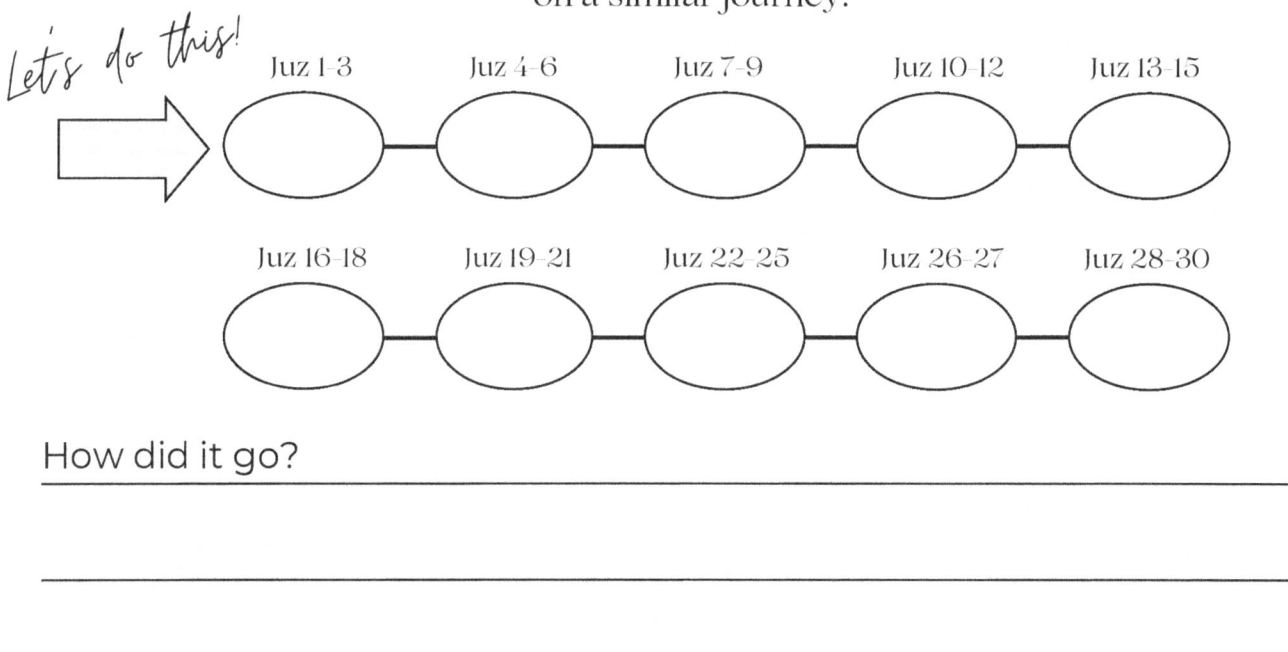

How did it go?

_____

_____

_____

What did I learn?

_____

_____

_____

10-Day Khatm (Completion) Qur'aan Tracker

Completing the Qur'aan in 10 Days:
A 10-day Qur'aan completion requires dedication and focus, making it an intense and spiritually uplifting endeavor. Each day involves reciting three Juz, immersing you deeply into the flow of the Qur'aan's powerful messages.

- "This is a month of striving," you remind yourself as you prioritize time for recitation above all else. Imagine completing the Qur'aan not once, but three times during Ramadhaan, multiplying the barakah and rewards.
- The Prophet Muhammad (peace be upon him) said: "The best of you are those who learn the Qur'aan and teach it." (Sahih al-Bukhari 5027) In this pursuit, you not only elevate your own faith but inspire others to embark on a similar journey.

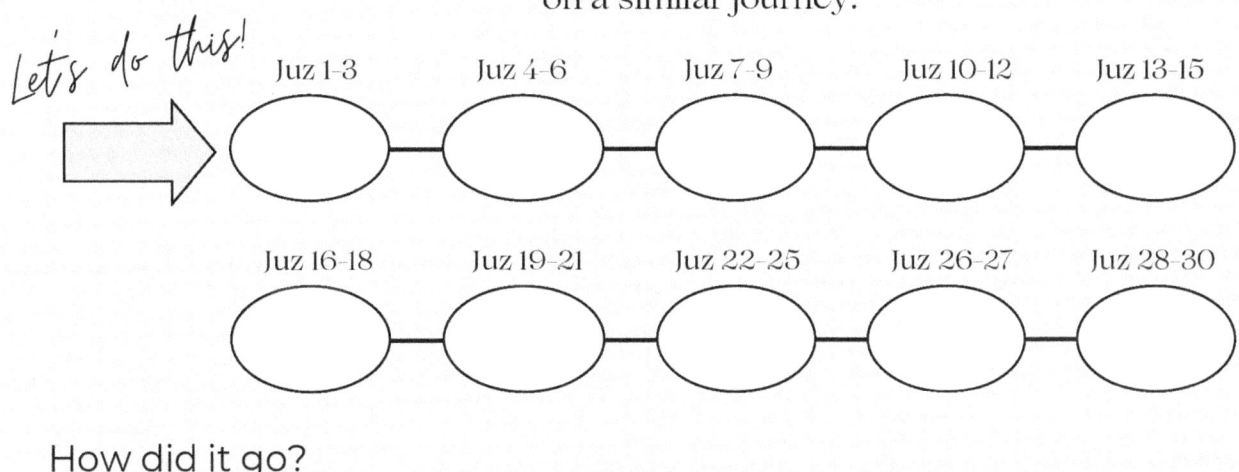

How did it go?
_____
_____
_____

What did I learn?
_____
_____
_____

10-Day Khatm (Completion) Qur'aan Tracker

Completing the Qur'aan in 10 Days:

A 10-day Qur'aan completion requires dedication and focus, making it an intense and spiritually uplifting endeavor. Each day involves reciting three Juz, immersing you deeply into the flow of the Qur'aan's powerful messages.

- "This is a month of striving," you remind yourself as you prioritize time for recitation above all else. Imagine completing the Qur'aan not once, but three times during Ramadhaan, multiplying the barakah and rewards.
- The Prophet Muhammad (peace be upon him) said: "The best of you are those who learn the Qur'aan and teach it." (Sahih al-Bukhari 5027) In this pursuit, you not only elevate your own faith but inspire others to embark on a similar journey.

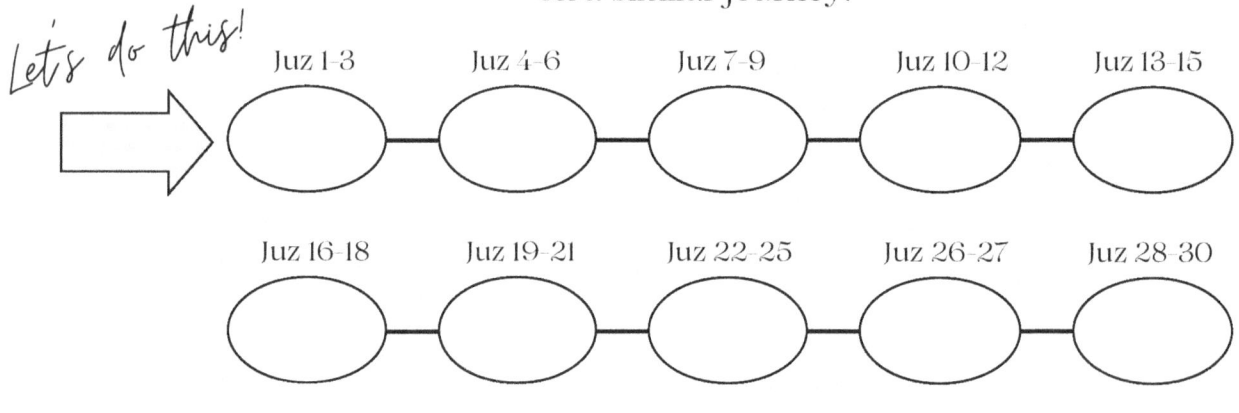

How did it go?
_____
_____
_____

What did I learn?
_____
_____
_____

10-Day Khatm (Completion) Qur'aan Tracker

Completing the Qur'aan in 10 Days:
A 10-day Qur'aan completion requires dedication and focus, making it an intense and spiritually uplifting endeavor. Each day involves reciting three Juz, immersing you deeply into the flow of the Qur'aan's powerful messages.

- "This is a month of striving," you remind yourself as you prioritize time for recitation above all else. Imagine completing the Qur'aan not once, but three times during Ramadhaan, multiplying the barakah and rewards.
- The Prophet Muhammad (peace be upon him) said: "The best of you are those who learn the Qur'aan and teach it." (Sahih al-Bukhari 5027) In this pursuit, you not only elevate your own faith but inspire others to embark on a similar journey.

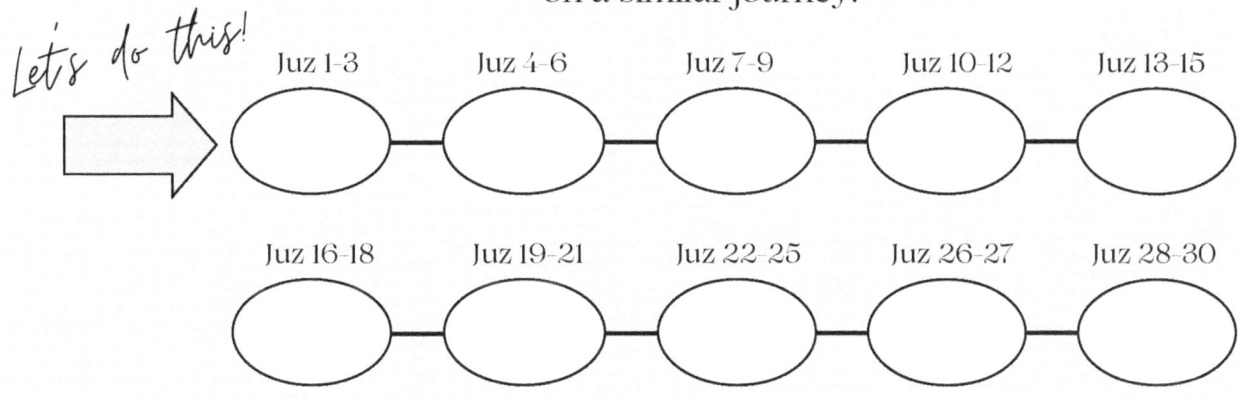

How did it go?
_____
_____
_____

What did I learn?
_____
_____
_____

10-Day Khatm (Completion) Qur'aan Tracker

Completing the Qur'aan in 10 Days:

A 10-day Qur'aan completion requires dedication and focus, making it an intense and spiritually uplifting endeavor. Each day involves reciting three Juz, immersing you deeply into the flow of the Qur'aan's powerful messages.

- "This is a month of striving," you remind yourself as you prioritize time for recitation above all else. Imagine completing the Qur'aan not once, but three times during Ramadhaan, multiplying the barakah and rewards.
- The Prophet Muhammad (peace be upon him) said: "The best of you are those who learn the Qur'aan and teach it." (Sahih al-Bukhari 5027) In this pursuit, you not only elevate your own faith but inspire others to embark on a similar journey.

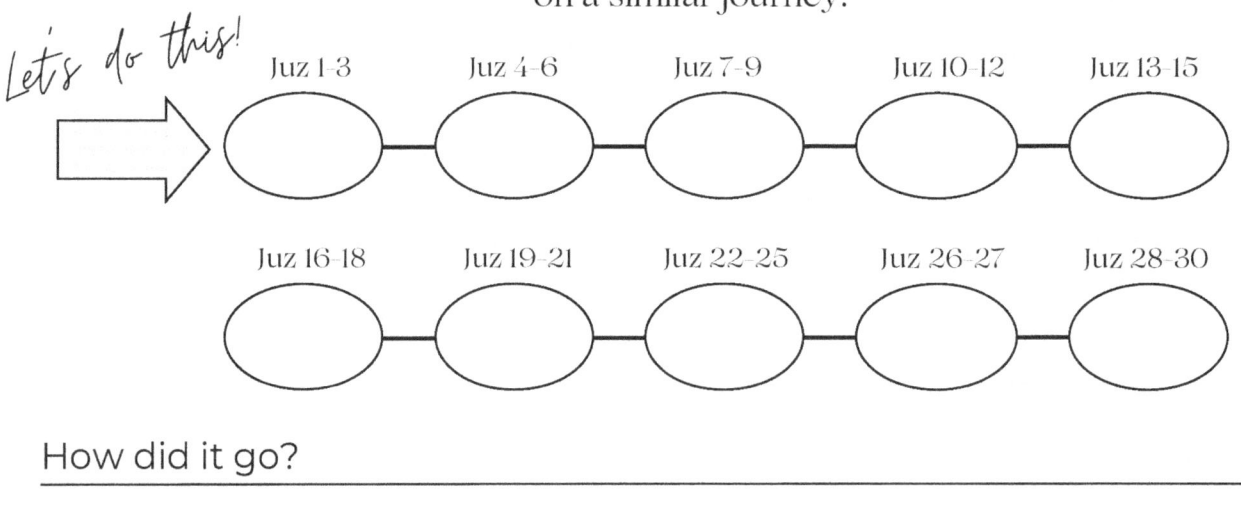

How did it go?

_____

_____

_____

What did I learn?

_____

_____

_____

The Qur'aan is not merely a book to be completed; it is a guide to be lived. As you journey through its chapters, strive to embody its teachings in your daily life. Make dua that Allaah allows the light of His words to illuminate your path and grant you steadfastness in carrying these lessons beyond Ramadhaan.

May your recitation be a source of joy, your reflections a source of clarity, and your efforts a source of reward in this life and the next. May Allaah make the Qur'aan the spring of your heart, the light of your chest, the evacuator of your grief and the remover of your distress. May Allaah grant you the best in this life and the next and allow you to be from the people of the Qur'aan and the people of Jannah. May the Peace & Blessing be upon our beloved Prophet Muhammad ﷺ, His Family & those that follow him Aameen.

www.ingramcontent.com/pod-product-compliance
Lightning Source LLC
Chambersburg PA
CBHW060306010526
44108CB00041B/2487